New Life For Health

The Commission was set up in March 1999 by the Association of Community Health Councils for England and Wales (ACHCEW) in order independently to examine the issue of the public interest, and how it is served by the system of accountability in the NHS. A full list of the Commissioners appears in Annex 1.

Will Hutton was appointed chief executive of the Industrial Society in February 2000. He was previously editor-in-chief of the *Observer*, and is the author of many books, including the bestselling *The State We're In*.

NEW LIFE FOR HEALTH

The Commission on the NHS chaired by Will Hutton

VINTAGE

Published by Vintage 2000

2 4 6 8 10 9 7 5 3 1

Copyright © Will Hutton 2000

First published in Great Britain by
Vintage 2000

Vintage
Random House, 20 Vauxhall Bridge Road, London SW1V 2SA

Random House Australia (Pty) Limited
20 Alfred Street, Milsons Point, Sydney,
New South Wales 2061, Australia

Random House New Zealand Limited
18 Poland Road, Glenfield,
Auckland 10, New Zealand

Random House (Pty) Limited
Endulini, 5A Jubilee Road, Parktown 2193, South Africa

The Random House Group Limited Reg. No. 954009

www.randomhouse.co.uk

A CIP catalogue record for this book
is available from the British Library

ISBN 0099285754

Papers used by Random House are natural, recyclable
products made from wood grown in sustainable forests. The
manufacturing processes conform to the environmental
regulations of the country of origin

Set in 10½/12 Sabon by SX Composing DTP, Rayleigh, Essex
Printed and bound in Great Britain by
Cox & Wyman Ltd, Reading, Berkshire

CONTENTS

ACKNOWLEDGEMENTS

An ambitious report of this kind is impossible without the contribution of many people to whom we are indebted. We are intensely grateful to all those who responded to our call for evidence, both written and oral (we enclose a full list in Annex 6). Thanks are due also to the Joseph Rowntree Reform Trust for its grant to support our opinion poll, and to Professor Patrick Dunleavy of the LSE, Nick Sparrow of ICM, and Stuart Weir for drawing up the poll questionnaire and analysing the results. Susan Kerrison of the School of Public Policy at UCL made an invaluable contribution in her work on complaints procedures. Any mistakes are ours. And last but not least, thanks to the School of Public Policy for making rooms available for more than twenty meetings and hearings.

We would also like to thank Angeline Burke and Frances Presley for their administrative, research and secretarial back-up. As chairman, I want to thank every Commission member for the way they all drafted and commented upon the innumerable drafts and redrafts – a collegiate and accountable effort in every way. Thanks to my father for once again coming up with the title. And of course to my family, who suffered a distracted father yet again.

Will Hutton, April 2000

EXECUTIVE SUMMARY

THE NHS IS BRITAIN'S greatest and most prized national institution. The 1946 Act that created it declared that its aim was 'to deliver free and equal access to comprehensive health care: not to this or that sectional interest, but to the requirements of the British public as a whole'. At one stroke the then Labour government created a milestone in relieving one of the keenest fears of the great majority of the British people – of being unable to afford proper health care – and in establishing the cornerstone of social citizenship in Britain. In 1951 ministers acknowledged that the NHS was 'the most popular of all our new institutions'.

More than fifty years later, the NHS retains its national mandate and its popularity. A special poll we commissioned to inform this report found that the great majority of people – nearly two-thirds (63 per cent) – regard the NHS as the 'most valuable institution' in this country, easily surpassing in public regard the runners-up: Parliament (12 per cent) and the police (11 per cent). (Only 3 per cent put the Royal Family first.)*

The NHS is tasked to provide equal care to every British citizen on the basis of their equal need, irrespective of where they live or how much they earn. The service is publicly

---

*ICM Research interviewed a random sample of 1,004 adults aged 18 or over by telephone between 24 and 26 March 2000. Interviews were conducted across the country and the results have been weighted to the profile of all adults. The poll was funded by the Joseph Rowntree Reform Trust as part of its 'State of the Nation' polling programme.

1

owned and accountable, and is almost wholly financed by general taxation. Ever since its foundation it has commanded extraordinary popular affection and loyalty. Its medical and non-medical staff alike have been strongly committed to its success and values. Indeed they have been one of the NHS's strongest and most enduring assets.

However, a gap has opened up both between what the NHS is able to deliver and the expectations and needs of its users, and between its original principles and current practice. The UK has slipped to almost the bottom of OECD countries with respect to public funding and levels of health service provision. The capacity of individual patients and local communities to secure the health care they want and expect, to win information about the reasons for decisions and to pursue complaints according to basic principles of natural justice are poor. By any standard – ranging from relief from cancer to long-term care and rehabilitation – Britain's system of public and clinical health care is unsatisfactory.

These trends have been clear for some time, but over the last five years there is growing evidence that they have now reached a critical point. Indeed it was the political impossibility of not responding to deeply felt public criticism that provoked the government into its announcement in the March 2000 Budget of a sustained and substantial increase in NHS spending over the next four years, along with the Prime Minister's earlier aspiration to lift British health spending to the EU average. The leading professional organisations within the NHS have become less restrained in their complaints about the standards of clinical care they are able to offer, the pressure on services and beds and the intractability of waiting lists. The poor pay and working conditions for NHS workers are greatly resented, and there are signs that the turnover rates among some categories of staff are dangerously high. The public is less willing to accept indifferent standards, the number of complaints is rising, and there is an ominous rise in the cumulative potential bill for medical negligence – on the latest figures close to £3 billion.

The ICM poll reveals considerable public concern about the service the the NHS provides. Only 4 per cent of people think that the NHS provides a good service that cannot be improved, while a third agree that it 'basically provides a good service' that could be improved in small ways. However nearly two-thirds believe that it requires to be improved 'quite a lot' (43 per cent) or that it delivers a poor service and 'needs a great deal of improvement' (19 per cent).

There are three main reasons for the disturbing deterioration in service. First, the NHS has been kept on short financial rations since its foundation, notwithstanding the overwhelming public support for the institution. Governments have sought to contain costs by redefining what the NHS provides, so eroding the principles of comprehensive care and services free at the point of delivery. There has been too little focus on benefits and an over-emphasis on cost control. A growing number of services – NHS dentistry, optical services, some routine elective care and the majority of long-term care services – can no longer be regarded as being provided universally, freely and equally. Individuals have increasingly been left to fund them themselves. Within the NHS rationing has spread together with inequity as the rationing criteria have varied between health authorities and health service providers. At the same time, due to underfunding, there has been a consistent inability to raise levels of care and treatment in line with the public's rise in living standards and its accompanying expectations.

In this respect the government's promise that NHS spending will rise by 6.1 per cent annually in real terms over the next four years is a welcome change of course, as is the aspiration to lift spending towards the EU average, although we note that even after the promised increase in spending it will still fall some way short of that aim. But for the first time since its foundation the chronic underfunding of the NHS is likely to be at least partially addressed. How that money is spent, however, and the manner in which the government is making reciprocal demands for NHS modernisation and improved outcomes, only increases the urgency of addressing the other shortcomings that our report discusses.

The second reason is closely related to the first. Important inequalities have followed the introduction of the 'internal market', for paradoxically it was so poorly designed that it produced the disadvantages of markets with none of their advantages – even if those had been appropriate for the health service, which we doubt. Aiming to devolve decision-making and responsibility to promote efficient resource allocation, the new structure exacerbated inequalities through introducing market-based contracting between local NHS providers and fund- and non-fund-holding GPs and thus moving away from the principle of equity and community risk-sharing. The 'internal market' created winners and losers, among purchasers, providers and patients alike.

The current Labour government recognises these deficiencies, but its 1999 Health Act only partially addresses the problem because the new system of commissioning promises to reproduce some of the damaging fragmentation caused by the 'internal market'. The financing of new replacement hospital construction through the Private Finance Initiative (PFI) has tended to reduce bed numbers and clinical staff budgets by up to 30 and 25 per cent respectively in the areas to be served by newly constructed PFI hospitals. Care and clinical priorities are now explicitly traded off against economic goals, including returns to private shareholders.

Primary care has long been the Achilles heel of the NHS. Unlike the rest of the medical profession GPs retained their independent contractor status after 1948, but despite being entirely dependent on public funds, structures to ensure direct public accountability at local level have been lacking. The new Primary Care Groups (PCGs) and Primary Care Trusts (PCTs), which are to run integrated, unified budgets for the total health care in local areas, do little to reduce the accountability deficit, even though one of their purported aims is to delegate decision-making to local level, and ultimately PCTs will have a majority of lay persons on their boards. The establishment of the National Institute for Clinical Excellence (NICE) and the Commission for Health Improvement (CHI) is meant to level up varying standards in clinical treatment and to ensure that local health policies correspond to best practice. But they are superimposed upon structures and systems that at least in part pull in the opposite direction.

4

The third reason for the shortfall in service is that the doctrine of ministerial accountability has disguised a wider absence of accountability and transparency of decision-making within NHS structures. The Commission is concerned that the government and NHS are not accountable enough across the gamut of decision-making on health care – from the overall level of funding and planning of services, to the redress of individual patients' grievances and the say they have in their medical treatment. More than half the public (55 per cent) believe that patients should have 'a lot of power' over the medical treatment they receive, and a further 39 per cent that they should have 'a little power'. But only one in five people (20 per cent) actually believe that they have a lot of power over the treatment they receive and as many say they have no power at all. About half think they have 'a little power'. So although doctors and medical staff increasingly attempt to consult and inform their patients, there is clearly room for a more empowering ethos in the NHS.

The absence of accountability has coincided with the increasing insistence, in all walks of British life, on more accountability, more information and higher standards in decision-making and subsequent execution. The NHS is inevitably exposed to the full force of these developing trends. The government is seeking to address such new demands from the public by calling for improved professional regulation, establishing NICE and CHI, and adherence to the Patients Charter. NHS Direct and walk-in centres are also part of an attempt to recognise that citizens are becoming more active consumers of health, as the NHS Alliance put it their discussion paper published in March.* But these initiatives cannot close the accountability deficit.

In the absence of adequate, strong democratic structures the public is using the NHS's undeveloped complaint mechanisms or even the courts to seek redress of grievances – a development that is bound to grow further when the 1998

---

*NHS Alliance, *Implementing the Vision: Maintaining the Values*. NHS Alliance: 2000. The NHS Alliance was formerly the National Association of Commissioning GPs.

Human Rights Act becomes operational in autumn this year. Together these trends raise the risk that litigants could exercise a disproportionate influence over policy and could undermine the capacity for rational, collective decision-making that ought to be at the heart of the NHS.

The Commission is alarmed that the Prime Minister's strategy for driving improvements through the NHS is highly centralised. Incorporating small appointed task forces at the centre will compound the inherent weaknesses of the service. The NHS is too large and complex an institution to be controlled effectively from the centre, with even the outgoing chief executive, Alan Langlands, conceding that the control of the NHS has foundered on an over-reliance on the contractual relationship between health authorities and trusts that obliges the NHS Executive's regional offices to adopt a hands-off approach. There is an urgent need for more local account-ability rather than yet more administrative fiats from the top. A democratic voice and accountability must be deployed as buttresses against inequality and inefficiency of provision. In our view, democratic accountability at all levels of the service will be a more effective means of supplying the discipline that the Prime Minister is seeking to impose at and from the top.

For the chief route in a democracy towards closing what amounts to a gap in trust between the public, the government and the NHS is to promote the accountability of this great institution and thereby secure its legitimacy. The more the public are directly involved in running the NHS, even in electing its decision-makers, the more accountable the NHS will become, and the more the public's sense of ownership and its legitimacy will grow. The public will then share in the crucial decisions over funding, both nationally and locally.

The public must mean all of the public, including women, people with disabilities and the ethnic minority communities. In the wake of the Lawrence inquiry in which the government accepted that there is racism in all our institutions, we need to build an NHS that is explicitly committed to the promotion of equality: from its system of governance to how staff are recruited, developed, promoted and retained.

The poor levels of accountability within the NHS have been debated ever since its launch, but the issue has never been resolved. In general, under the tradition of ministerial responsibility, the secretary of state or minister responsible for health is made accountable to the public via the House of Commons. This approach has changed slightly with devolution, and in Scotland and Wales their own health ministers take a measure of responsibility, though overall health spending is still largely set by the Treasury. But, mainly due to the weakness of the House of Commons, the tradition of ministerial responsibility has long been shown to be incapable of delivering real accountability (see chapter 3).*

Over the NHS's history there have been a variety of regimes in which decision-making has been delegated to regional and local level, with a varying readiness to incorporate external voices and assert some degree of accountability, but no settled system has been established. In addition there are ad hoc independent inquiries and review panels in response to individual problems and public concerns, and there is a complaints procedure for individual cases. But none are backed by a constitutionally entrenched framework of patient rights.

Over the past year, the Commission has considered how best to remedy the shortfalls in accountability, ranging from the overall decision-making apparatus of the service, its rationing processes and the role of the courts, to the work of health authorities and the new primary care groups at local level. At present there is only one formal mechanism for giving voice to the concerns of patients and families – the 206 Community Health Councils (CHCs) in England and Wales and the 16 Local Health Councils in Scotland (Northern Ireland has four health and social services councils). The CHCs and their Scottish equivalents act as formal watchdogs

---

*It is widely recognised that the House of Commons is dominated by the executive and that ministerial responsibility to Parliament is largely a constitutional fiction. See, for example, Marr A. *Ruling Britannia*, Michael Joseph: 1995; Woodhouse, D. *Ministers and Parliament: Accountability in Theory and Practice*, Clarendon Press, Oxford: 1994.

and represent patients' interests. Recent structural changes have removed the regional health authorities and downgraded the district health authorities with which CHCs and Scottish Health Boards and local councils have had a statutory monitoring role and rights to be consulted.

In the Commission's view, the overall system of accountability in the NHS is unacceptably weak. It is perhaps the least accountable of Britain's major public institutions, even though access to health is the prime concern of British citizens. This democratic deficit in the NHS has been widened by recent changes to its structure and is likely to widen still further as the next round of structural change takes effect and the highly centralised strategy to raise standards commences. We have come to agree with the Select Committee on Health, which in autumn 1999 argued that the NHS needed to transform an ethos that is too defensive, inward-looking, and locked in a blame culture.* However, the scale of this change means more than new ministerial initiatives, new quangos and task forces, cosmetic additions to practice and regulation and more codes and charters, all lubricated by more cash. Something more fundamental is required.

As we have seen, the NHS is a highly valued national institution. In our poll the public also showed a remarkable attachment to its basic founding principle – the idea that people should have access to 'free medical treatment at the time of need'. The people polled agreed almost unanimously (96 per cent) that this should become a right under a British Bill of Rights, ranking this right to free medical treatment at the time of need with other basic human rights, such as those of free speech, fair jury trial and privacy. Thus our chief recommendation is that the government should consult the public over writing a constitution for the NHS to ensure that this founding principle is protected in practice by the govern-

---

*Procedures Related to Adverse Clinical Incidents and Outcomes in Medical Care: sixth report, session 1998–9. Vol. 1: Report and proceedings of the Committee. David Hinchcliffe. House of Commons Health Committee. London: Stationery Office, 1999. HC 549–1. See p. xxiii.

ment and NHS. This constitution should represent the shared principles and values to which the public, all political parties and NHS constituencies subscribe. We also recommend that the government should establish the NHS as a national institution, independent of direct government control, and reform these structures to give practical shape to its constitutional independence.

There are models for such an arm's-length institution, though they are less ambitious in scale and suffer some shortcomings. For example, the BBC is a public corporation with its own 'constitution' – that is, its royal charter. The Bank of England has been given independence with a remit set by government ministers. However the purpose of these arrangements in both cases is to offer these institutions some protection from government interference and to remove their operations from the daily round of Britain's intense and confrontational party politics. Our aim should be to do better with the NHS.

We do not suggest that the NHS should or could become wholly independent of government and the political process. The public choose governing parties at elections to rule the country and hand over responsibility for the NHS and other major services to those parties; and they have the power to remove them from government at a subsequent election should they fail to discharge their responsibilities. Thus it is entirely proper that the government, through the cabinet and secretary of state, should determine the policies of the NHS and set the level of resources the service requires. Our proposals do not subvert those basic provisions of Britain's political system. Our poll shows considerable public support for the idea of an NHS constitution. We gave respondents a choice between giving the NHS a constitution of its own 'to define the government's duty to deliver free medical care at a time when people require it', and trusting 'elected politicians in government to safeguard the NHS's performance of its duty to the public'. Nearly three-quarters (69 per cent) said that the NHS needed a constitution; a quarter (26 per cent) put their trust in government ministers. We believe that the balance we recommend between the overall authority of government and an arm's-length NHS with a constitution of its own fairly reflects the public view.

Under our proposals, government ministers would be required in future to frame policies and allocate resources subject to the provisions of the NHS constitution. The service itself could be removed from within the Department of Health, where it is currently situated, and transformed into an independent institution, either as a public corporation, like the BBC and Bank of England, or as a major quango or executive agency, or as an elected body. We are aware that some executive agencies and public corporations are no more transparent in their decision-making than departments of state, but one of the advantages of our proposed constitution is that it would make openness a constitutional requirement. This new NHS would be charged with carrying out government policies within the resources allocated, but the whole process of deciding policies, allocating and using resources, and delivering care and services, would be made transparent instead of being contained within the opaque processes of a government department; and the constitution would provide a framework for the aims and purposes of the service.

Parliament would continue to play its role, keeping government policy under scrutiny, examining and amending legislation on the NHS, and calling government to account, but its role would be strengthened by the constitution and the new transparency that an independent institution would bring about. A fully resourced Select Committee for Health, also strengthened by the introduction of the constitution, would become its first custodian; and the Health Ombudsman could be required to report to this committee as well as to the Committee on Public Administration. In this way the health select committee would take on an enhanced role holding the newly independent NHS accountable to parliamentary and public opinion.

We see the NHS constitution as entrenching and extending the concept of social citizenship and a wider view of the public interest in the health service. We believe our proposal builds on and improves the current developments in Britain's governing arrangements, with the widespread establishment of executive agencies to create more independent, transparent and efficient delivery of public services, and the newly independent Bank of England with its power to set interest rates but accountable to the Treasury Select Committee and the public through the publication of its monthly minutes. The constitution will create genuine independence and transparency, a standard that most public bodies do not meet. The proposal will also complement the moves made by professional regulators within the service, such as the General Medical Council (GMC) and UK Central Council of Nursing, Midwifery and Health Visiting (UKCC) to improve their oversight and incorporate lay representation on their decision-making councils. The defects of the GMC's processes have been exposed to public view in dramatic fashion in the Bristol and Shipman cases; in future, the public could be reassured by the fact that the GMC and other professional regulators would have to act under obligations set by the NHS and an extended legal mandate.

Moreover the proposal also goes with the grain of moves to decentralise decision-making to British regions and smaller governing units which are more responsive to regional and local opinion. And it offers a way out of the stale debate over how both to increase the resources flowing to the NHS and to improve their deployment. By re-establishing trust and increasing the transparency with which new cash is used, the constitution will serve to legitimise increased taxation as the means to fund the NHS. It also offers a means to break the excessive preoccupation with cost control to allow a much more sophisticated public debate about costs and associated benefits in which a better-informed public with entrenched rights to information, complaint and redress can balance and discuss the merits of increased spending with improved health care. Equality of access to health will become legally binding; the need to ensure equality of treatment regardless of age, gender or race would be a constitutional requirement. The gross inequalities of postcode prescribing and the worst results of some PFI contracts would be constitutionally forbidden. Complaints and oversight procedures, ranging from the status of CHCs to the powers of the ombudsman, can be vastly strengthened and constitutionally entrenched.

In summary we recommend that:

- The NHS should be given a constitution to protect its founding principles and give positive shape to government policies and its own practice.
- The NHS should become a public corporation at arm's length from government with its own board and operational freedom.
- The NHS should be made democratic and accountable at local and regional level; locally through transforming health authorities into elected bodies with a measure of appointment for the sake of expertise and balance, and eventually at regional level through regional assemblies in England as well as the Scottish Parliament and assemblies in Wales and Northern Ireland. As an interim measure in England, regional accountability should rest with the new indirectly elected regional chambers as they come into being.
- NHS trusts should be made accountable to representative health authorities locally, or to more representative versions of the new Primary Care Groups (PCGs) and Primary Care Trusts (PCTs).
- The public should be given a right of access to all meetings, minutes and policy papers of all executive and advisory public bodies within the NHS, subject to the protection of individual privacy.
- Within a diverse multi-ethnic community the NHS should make an explicit commitment to the promotion of equality to its system of governance, provision of health care and treatment of staff.
- The value judgements determining the NHS's efficiency and use of resources should be explicitly opened up to public scrutiny through the availability of all information determining financial and budgetary decision-making.
- Lay representation on the new PCGs and PCTs should be strengthened, perhaps by way of election by the relevant patient body, and they should serve populations that

are geographically contiguous with health authority boundaries.

- All appointments to NHS trusts, PCGs and PCTs should be advertised and made by nomination committees established by representative health authorities, and their representation should reflect the whole community.
- The network of community health councils should be strengthened by extra central public funding and an enhanced statutory role as patient watchdogs and advocates.
- All complaints from patients and their families should be handled by genuinely independent review panels.
- The Select Committee on Health should be strengthened by adequate financial and staff resources.
- The Health Ombudsman should have the powers to inquire into policy issues and to initiate inquiries under clear criteria, with sufficient resources to follow up his recommendations.
- Substantial lay representation should be introduced by law into all the regulatory agencies including the new Care Standards Commission, General Medical Council and all the professional associations, royal colleges and other bodies that set standards of care and provide training for health professionals and workers and regulate private providers.
- To ensure a genuinely transparent health service, the Freedom of Information Bill should be amended to open up government policy-making to public scrutiny and the Commissioner for Open Government should be given the power to investigate and overrule official refusals to provide information.
- All independent contractors and private health providers must subscribe to the same rules of oversight, transparency, inspection and accountability as public bodies within the NHS.
- The Patients Charter should become part of the NHS's core constitution.

We believe that taken together these reforms will transform the accountability of the NHS and the transparency of decision-making. They will reorient the NHS in a new principled direction, so recovering its sense of purpose and idealism. They will entrench equality and accountability into the bedrock of the organisation. They will rebuild the relationship between the public, patients, doctors and NHS staff, and government, on a new basis of openness and therefore trust. We believe that they will be widely welcomed by the medical professions because at the same time they will expose the trade-offs and financial constraints within which doctors and carers now have to operate. By establishing a process of open negotiation between government and the NHS for funds, the hidden rationing and open inequities will become subject to full public oversight and thus properly inform the national debate about the funding of the NHS – an issue that although beyond the remit of this Commission is central to its future.

Our proposals should not be seen as a final blueprint. The proposed constitution should only be finalised after widespread public debate and representation by every interested party. There is a case for a further full-scale inquiry: to examine the future shape of the civil service and the appropriate mechanisms for its accountability. We recognise that the proposal for elected representation at local and regional level (and even possibly at national level) will be seen as controversial in some quarters. However, there is considerable support for more democratic health authorities locally, both within the NHS (as evidence to the Commission indicates) and among the general public. Our poll shows majority support for elected, or partly elected, partly appointed, local health authorities rather than the existing government-appointed bodies or making local health care a responsibility of local government (see chapter 7).

Once we accept the principle of a constitution and a democratic NHS, it is difficult to see how key decision-making functions should be made accountable to the public other than through elected representatives. Some of our detailed proposals are echoed in other recent reports, notably by the Select Committee on Health, the National Consumer Council and the NHS Alliance. Overall our ideas are fully consistent with the recommendations of the Council of Europe that patients be fully involved in health decision-making. They will not be the last word, but they do provide a starting point for discussion about how to create a modern, efficient and truly responsive health service that meets the demands of the British public.

The Commission was established in March 1999 by the Association of Community Health Councils for England and Wales (ACHCEW) in order to examine the issue of the public interest and accountability in the NHS. Although launched by ACHCEW it is fully independent, and its mandate has offered it a wide remit. Our terms of reference are: 'In recognising that the ultimate purpose of the NHS is to serve the public interest, to identify the ways in which that public interest can best be served by the achievement of a full and effective system of accountability'. (See Annex 1 for membership of the Commission.)

I

FIRST PRINCIPLES

THE NHS EXISTS to serve the public interest. Our Commission was set up 'to identify the ways in which that public interest can best be served by the achievement of a full and effective system of public accountability'.

But what is the public interest? The answer to this question probably seemed unproblematic to the founders of the NHS, but the Britons of the first decade of the new millennium are no longer the united people of the immediate aftermath of the Second World War. The United Kingdom has been under internal and external pressure to free up its constitution, opening its borders to international interests while simultaneously partially freeing up the peoples of Scotland, Wales and Northern Ireland so that they can assert their own interests separately from Britain's central government. England's regions are also quietly raising their own potentially autonomous voices. We live in a time of flux, when the very idea of the collective British consciousness manifested in an uncontroversial vision of the public interest lacks conviction. At times, the country seems more like a collection of disparate interest groups lobbying for sectional interests than a nation speaking with a single voice.

But while finding an easy consensus on precisely where the public interest lies is no longer straightforward, the public consensus on retaining the NHS is as firm as ever. Along with the BBC and one or two other beacons of excellence, the NHS has so grown on the British people that it now helps to define our identity. At a time of rampant change elsewhere, the public commitment in Britain to the NHS has been an unwavering, uncompromising and (for some politicians) deeply inconvenient political fact. Public support for the NHS transcends sectional, regional or national quarrels, reflecting evidence of a strong consensus on certain basic values.

Underlying values of the NHS

Section 1(1) of the pioneering 1946 Act that established the NHS declared that it 'shall be the duty of the Minister of Health . . . to promote the establishment in England and Wales of a comprehensive health service designed to secure improvement in the physical and mental health of the people of England and Wales and the prevention, diagnosis and treatment of illness, and for that purpose to provide or secure the effective provision of services in accordance with the following provisions of this Act'. The Scottish NHS Act in 1947 made the same statutory commitment (see section 1 (1)). In introducing the bill to the House of Commons on 30 April 1946, the Secretary of State for Health, Aneurin Bevan, described the measure as devoted 'not to this or that sectional interest, but to the requirements of the British public as a whole' (HC Debs, 30 April 1946, col. 43). When the NHS was formally established, the government sent a leaflet to every home in the land proclaiming in ringing terms the outcome it had set out to achieve: It will provide you with all medical, dental and nursing care. Everyone rich or poor, man woman or child, can use it or any part of it. There are no charges, except for a few special items. There are no insurance qualifications. But it is not a charity. You are all paying for it, mainly as taxpayers, and it will relieve your money worries in time of illness (Webster, C. *The National Health Service: A Political History*, OUP 1998.).

Over time, these general statements have crystallised into three fundamental principles, which are still seen as defining the basic goals of the NHS, although everyone recognises that the performance does not always match the aspiration:

The NHS should be a universal service, efficiently providing a high standard of health care to the whole population.

The services of the NHS should be free at the point of delivery.

The delivery of the NHS services should be fair, with everyone's needs assessed on an equitable basis, regardless of their means, ethnicity, gender, age or any other difference.

We believe that these principles are accurate reflections of what the public expects from its National Health Service. It is also our opinion that they continue to provide the best available prescription for the health of our society. Variations of the principles are to be found in repeated ministerial statements, and in the definitions offered by professional and others working within the service. For example, in September 1997 the National Association of Commissioning GPs set out their vision as being 'to develop a comprehensive NHS that is fair to those who use it and those who work within it, efficient and effective in its use of resources, sensitive to the needs of individuals and communities and openly accountable for its actions' (*Restoring the Vision: Making Health the Incentive*). Our version of the NHS's guiding principles is bolstered by the opinion poll data which have been specially commissioned for this Report, with 96 per cent supporting the right to treatment at the time of need as a fundamental social right. In a MORI poll for *The Times* conducted in January 2000, 70 per cent of those asked rated health care as the most important issues facing Britain. The current government's 1997 election manifesto committed it to 'the historic principle: that if you are ill or injured there will be a national health service there to help; and access to it will be based on need and need alone – not on your ability to pay, or on who your GP happens to be or on where you live'.

Protecting the public interest

Having discussed the substantive principles that we feel should determine how the public interest is defined, we now turn to the procedures that might, as our terms of reference put it, lead to a 'full and effective system of public accountability'.

It is a systemic weakness of the NHS that it has never been a properly democratically accountable organisation. The Secretary of State for Health has served as a notionally accountable political leader, answerable directly to Parliament for the way the NHS is run, but even at its inception there was a degree of unreality about a concept of accountability that made the minister responsible, in Aneurin Bevan's phrase, even for the falling of a bedpan.

The world is now much more complex. If it was ever possible for a single minister to take responsibility for all that took place in the health service, it most certainly is not possible now. Moreover, as we have pointed out above, the doctrine of ministerial responsibility as an instrument of accountable government has been generally discredited in practice. It is still officially argued that it provides an effective way of securing accountability in the NHS, but it is widely recognised that the emperor has no clothes.

In our view, the drift away from an effective system of accountability is damaging not only to our democratic traditions but also to the efficiency of the NHS in its provision of health care. This flaw in the NHS democratic process has made it possible for the definition of the 'public interest' to be appropriated by institutions claiming an exclusive knowledge of what that interest involves, but which are only tenuously plugged in to public opinion. The NHS has been repeatedly stood on its head, not on the basis of healthy public debate, but through such stunted democratic outgrowths as a parliamentary dog-fight here, a television interview there, this statement by self-appointed health experts, that pressure group manifesto, or even a line or two in a party manifesto. The circumstances under which the 'internal market' was introduced into the NHS were breathtakingly irresponsible.

As things stand, a massive state framework incorporating a large bureaucracy and a plethora of nominated bodies monopolise the articulation of the public interest; 99 health authorities in England, some 400 NHS Trusts and some 480 PCGs. None of these bodies are elected. They all owe their patronage to a series of Secretaries of State and derive their legitimacy from the doctrine of parliamentary accountability. Major structural flaws in the NHS – its bureaucratic remoteness, its insensitivity to some individual needs, its recent flirtation with an ersatz conception of the market – can all arguably be traced to the insecurity of its democratic base.

We are not saying that there is no accountability in the NHS. On the contrary, a feature of recent reforms has been an explosion of systems of accountability, with doctors, nurses, managers and others within the system being increasingly required to meet targets, perform in certain acceptable ways and constantly explain and justify what they are doing. But this is the accountability of bureaucratic command and blame-allocation, not of democratic partnership. The modern NHS is constantly on the search for individuals responsible for its evident shortcomings. There is of course a place in any large organisation for just this kind of preventive and punitive control over staff. But proper democratic accountability is not about the search for a scapegoat, even a blameworthy one; it is about protecting the substantive goals, the underlying vision of the NHS, by involving the public in securing the service from destabilising influences and then in helping it towards a state of health as good as that which it seeks to guarantee its users.

We see the solution to this structural flaw in the NHS as lying in a thoroughgoing re-engineering of its institutions so as to fill the democratic vacuum that allows the substantive principles and goals of the NHS to be eroded through a lack of adequate public scrutiny and debate. The government recognises that something is missing when it observes that 'involving service users and carers is an important part of improving service quality in the NHS' (*Patient and Public Involvement in the new NHS*, Department of Health, 1999:1), but we argue that reforms need to go further than the government and managers of the NHS currently contemplate. We suggest that three basic procedural principles should be developed to protect the substantive principles for which the NHS was created, and to ensure that any deviation from these substantive principles is made only after open and democratic debate.

The procedural principles we propose are:

1 *Representative government.* As far as possible, decisions affecting the determination and maintenance of the public interest in the NHS should be made by elected representatives, and not by government nominees.

2 *Informed public debate.* The governance of the NHS should be open whenever patient confidentiality permits, both at the centre and in every NHS body. The formulation of policies should be informed by public debate before being crystallised in firm political proposals.

3 *Accountability.* Individuals, boards and groups within the NHS who make decisions should be held democratically accountable for their actions.

4 *Equality.* The governance, service delivery and employment practices of the NHS should recognise the diverse, multi-ethnic and multi-cultural nature of British society and should aim both to promote equality and to monitor equality outcomes.

Efficiency, funding and the public interest

Although our terms of reference do not extend to making recommendations over the level and character of NHS funding, debating whether health rationing is inevitable, or technically examining how clinical standards of health provision might be improved, it is obvious that these issues are closely related to the pursuit of the public interest in the NHS. We did not attempt to reach a consensus on these questions. However, there was a consensus that an improvement in the accountability of the NHS and transparency in its decision-making would radically transform the terms of public debate and expose the hidden value judgements that lie behind these arguments over the level and distribution of resources. It would thus greatly enhance the capacity to make judgements on such issues in the future.

For example, both compulsory private insurance and hypothecated taxes have been proposed as means of relieving the government from the politically difficult obligation of raising general tax rates in order to secure the public's desired standards of health provision. We regard organising the debate over future funding into these two opposing categories as a Hobson's choice. Private insurance in the United States is accompanied by unacceptable inequality and rising administrative costs. On the other hand hypothecated taxes, although superficially attractive, fluctuate with the economic cycle and after time necessarily become consolidated into general tax revenue as the 'extra' health care they pay for becomes the new baseline for care. Both alternatives are in our view undesirable, but they have achieved their prominence because the value judgements behind them have not been fully exposed, due to lack of reasoned information about the structure and growth of costs and benefits given the current lack of NHS accountability.

Instead of this distancing of the public from the profound value judgements that lie at the core of decision-making over funding, we believe it belongs at the forefront of electoral debate. However, voters cannot make rational decisions without reliable information. We therefore believe that there is a need to take the spin and dissimulation out of the reporting of NHS funding, so that what we see is what we get. At the same time, taxpayers need to be assured that their money is not being wasted.

Rationing is among the most contentious words in the NHS's lexicon. The apparently unremarkable claim that the demand for free health resources is likely to outstrip their supply, especially as medical technology advances and becomes relatively more expensive, has become laden with ideological overtones and value judgements. It is used to justify the further encouragement of private health insurance with the threat that otherwise the NHS will become an unsupportable 'burden' on the taxpayer. Alternatively, waiting lists are partially excused as an inevitable concomitant of free health. The counter-argument, that the public do not see taxation as a 'burden' but rather as the entry fee or membership insurance for a free, universal and equal health service and which they are willing to pay to avert substantive rationing, waiting lists and queues, is rarely mounted – even though every opinion poll finds that this is precisely the public's preference. A richer society can afford to pay proportionately and absolutely more for its health care, and technology offers substantial improvements in treatment and care. The implicit value judgements behind these varying positions need to be flushed out by democratic argument and engagement.

A parallel confusion arises over the question of 'efficiency', which again is a term that is seldom used objectively. In what sense should the NHS be efficient? In the current NHS, for example, myopic cost-cutting has led to an attempt to maximise patient throughput, with the result that there is inadequate spare bed capacity at times of high seasonal demand, as with the recent flu crisis. However, economic efficiency must not involve cutting costs without regard to the loss in benefit. On the contrary, no sensible discussion of efficiency is possible if only costs are considered. Explicit value judgements also need to be made about the benefits associated with alternative policies before their efficiency can be assessed. We believe that public participation in making such value judgements would greatly enhance the perceived legitimacy of the NHS.

In emphasising the importance of encouraging public participation in the value judgements necessary when allocating health benefits, we do not mean to suggest that the control of costs is not of considerable importance. However, even 'value for money' is a value-laden term, if used to reduce costs without regard for the consequent and unintended changes in the provision and distribution of benefits – hence the widespread condemnation of postcode prescribing and the like. Benefits need to be evaluated independently of costs before rational decisions can be made about what benefits the NHS can afford to provide. In summary, we believe that the evaluation of benefits should receive at least as much attention as the assessment of costs, and that the value judgements involved should be open, clear and explicit, so that the public knows what definition of the public interest the NHS is working with. Ultimately, the perceived legitimacy of the NHS depends on the extent to which this definition of the public interest meets with public approval. We believe that everybody, politicians included, would profit from opening up judgements on care and treatment priorities to the public and distancing them from party-political conflict.

2

SETTING THE SCENE

THE NHS IS the outstanding example of a successful public institution. However, it has suffered from under-funding throughout its history, and has never resolved the tensions over how it should be properly accountable to its users and the wider public. Formally, the Secretary of State for Health is responsible for running the NHS and making its policy in England, and in theory she or he is accountable to the House of Commons and, through MPs, to the electorate. Within the Department of Health, an NHS Executive is responsible for the day-to-day administration of the service. Senior civil servants at the Department of Health formally advise the Health Secretary and ministers on major decisions over health priorities, spending, pay and managerial issues, but in effect often take such decisions themselves. The Health Service Commissioner acts as an external ombudsman reporting to Parliament over complaints and best practice.

The National Audit Office and Audit Commission scrutinise the use of public funds by the NHS and carry out 'value for money' audits; and the NAO focuses parliamentary attention on its findings through regular reports to the Public Accounts Committee in the House of Commons. Under these arrangements, the Health Secretary alone is the formal guardian of the public interest in the NHS. The NHS is inevitably a complex body, and its complexities are multiplied by its close inter-relationship with the Department of Health. The NHS was once organised as a hierarchical command-and-control pyramid, with the NHS Executive at the centre within the Department, and then in descending order, regional and district health authorities (RHAs and DHAs). But Conservative governments shook this structure up in two rounds of reform in the early 1970s and again in the early 1990s. Regional health authorities were abolished and their role passed to government regional offices. District authorities survived these changes and still remain, but hospitals and other local services have been established as near autonomous 'NHS bodies' under nominated boards. NHS Trusts are public corporations responsible for the provision of health services. In theory, these bodies are responsible to the health authorities which act as 'purchasers' of their services within the 'internal market'.

The current government has stated that it intends to abolish the internal market. However, its reforms allow for the retention of purchasers and providers, public corporations and contracting mechanisms. It has also retained a capital charging system structured so that local NHS Trusts have to prioritise and fund their own investment, so that investment strategies vary considerably from trust to trust. Moreover, it has established a new set of local bodies, Primary Care Groups and Trusts (PCGs and PCTs), comprising local GPs (independent self-employed contractors) and representatives of local health service staffs, which will in effect take over the health authorities' 'purchasing' role. They are to commission health care on a contractual basis, so that much of the character of the 'internal market' is intended to remain. Like NHS trusts they are responsible to health authorities, with a health authority representative and a lay representative nominated by the health authority.

Outside the direct service lines of command there are a number of executive and advisory quangos that also play a role in providing and regulating health care. The National Institute for Clinical Excellence (NICE), recently established to ensure that best clinical practice is extended nationally, now looks like being a prime instrument of the government's strategy for raising standards, while Health Improvement Programmes (HImPs) are to be the main mechanism by which Health Authorities, Local Authorities, Trusts, PCGs and

PCTs develop local health strategies, taking into account the views and priorities of local people, local businesses and other local interests. The Commission for Health Improvement is tasked to scrutinise and monitor these programmes to ensure their effectiveness.

However, none of these bodies is accountable to the public through election. The members of their boards are all appointed. They are all supposedly accountable to the Secretary of State, who is in turn supposedly accountable for their activities and policies in the House of Commons. Though NHS quangos are subject to Nolan rules on appointments, the report of the commissioner for appointments in March showed that undue political manipulation can still take place.*

Outside these official structures, the courts play an increasing role through the legal processes of judicial review, under which the decisions of the Secretary of State, medical staff and officials may be subject to judicial scrutiny to ensure that their actions are reasonable, fair and unbiased. Further, professional bodies such as the General Medical Council, the Royal Colleges and others set standards for their professions and exercise discipline over them, although, as we detail in chapter 5, with inadequate powers and lay representation.

Scotland and Wales have won powers with devolution to decide on different health priorities from Westminster, but within an overall 'block' allocation of spending decided by the Treasury. In addition Scotland has the power to introduce primary health legislation. The arrangements in Northern Ireland have yet to be finalised, pending the establishment of the new constitutional settlement.

These arrangements mean that the public and interested parties can only seek to influence the policies and resources of the NHS by making representations to the single person responsible for the public interest in the NHS – the Secretary of State for Health. Yet while overall spending decisions are made centrally, under the ultimate control of the Treasury, decisions on policies and resource allocations are actually

---

*Dame Rennie Fritchie, *Public Appointments to NHS Trusts and Health Authorities*. www.ocpa.gov.uk.

made by the NHS executive within the Department of Health, by officials in the Department's regional offices, and within broad parameters by health authorities locally, a role which will be increasingly assumed by PCGs and PCTs. This results in, for example, the inequities thrown up by postcode prescribing, where eligibility for treatment depends on the budget and priorities of the health authority area where a person happens to live.

The twin impact of a greater consumer activism towards health together with the fragmentation and inequity of provision has made the public more ready to debate whether the right decisions are being made, and to challenge them when it considers they are not. The growing tendency to speak up has risen in part from deep trends in British society and culture: individuals are much more ready to challenge authority, to insist on redress of grievances and to resort to law to pursue their rights. No longer can doctors, clinicians, health managers and politicians decide what they consider to be the public interest in health behind closed doors with only nominal consultation, and expect their decisions to remain unchallenged.

This trend interacts with a growing insistence that health care must represent the best available practice. Whether in faulty cancer screening or surgical mishaps, the public is no longer willing to be docile about medical mistakes. It wants compensation, and bad doctors struck off the register. It wants proper investigation of mistakes, and recommendations about reformed procedures to be visibly and rapidly pursued. Patients are increasingly willing to protest about poor care – ranging from admissions procedures to treatment and convalescence. The judgements of health professionals and ministers are being challenged and increasingly contested in areas ranging from gender reassignment to cancer treatment.

The rapid pace of pharmaceutical, technological and surgical development has opened up new medical possibilities and increased the cost pressures upon the NHS. A richer population, while remaining profoundly attached to the NHS as a public institution, expects to see public health care matching its original principles over a widening range of care, and the same standards and choice that are available in the private sector. But the public does not view private insurance or privatisation of health care as desirable alternatives to the tax-financed NHS. Angus Reid, a Canadian polling firm, in a poll of 17 countries in February 2000 showed that Britain was unique in that a majority were in favour of paying higher tax to ensure better public services – a result that has been reflected in a series of polls over the last decade. Until this March's Budget this public preference had not been reflected in government policy. However, the current government's commitment to raise real health expenditure by more than 6 per cent annually in real terms over the next four years – so that as a proportion of GDP it will approach the European average – is the first responsive governmental approach to funding for more than twenty years.

There is growing concern about health inequalities. The root cause of these inequalities is to be found in the wider inequalities of society, but the power of major corporate interests, like the pharmaceutical industry, and some lobby groups often determines NHS priorities to the detriment of less powerful sections of society. A few powerful drug companies work closely with government health officials and have a major influence on clinical priorities and treatments. Drug companies also reach doctors in general practice regularly through advertisements and other means and are directly and indirectly represented on important quangos, such as the Committee for the Safety of Medicines and the Medicines Commission.

Sometimes their exercise of power is overt. The drug company Pfizer, for example, recently successfully challenged the capacity of the Health Secretary to issue blanket instructions to GPs to stop them from prescribing Viagra. Instead such instructions now have to be legally executed by changing regulations to schedule the drug.

Single-issue lobby groups also manage to influence the service's priorities and often to secure scarce resources while other areas – mental health, for example – are neglected and under-resourced. Health experience has always been closely related to income, but the current levels of income inequality are now generating widening health inequalities. It is well established that the middle classes benefit most from the clinical and other care that the NHS offers, as well as being generally more healthy than less well-off groups in society. Yet at the same time the service benefits from their more demanding and critical evaluation of its standards of care. One of the dangers of the current degree of under-funding, if continued, is that the growing number of private operations, except for acute services, threatens to leave the NHS increasingly as a second-rate rump. The middle class is beginning to give up on it, raising questions about how long it can maintain its position as a genuine universal public service.

These are not the only concerns the government must satisfy. There is a growing range of high-visibility issues with health implications ranging from the recent BSE crisis to the debate over the potential dangers of genetically modified foods. Such issues are typically handled by government officials and unelected quangos operating behind closed doors. The difficulty is that the government is suffering the obverse of the accountability and legitimacy gap: its assurances and those of its quango experts are simply no longer believed or trusted on such issues, and the judgements of government scientists are disputed. One beneficial outcome of giving the public full access to the work of quangos is that their expert recommendations and advice may gain public trust.

In short, a health-care gap has opened up between government and citizen that urgently needs to be closed. The NHS needs to be more accountable, not just to improve its legitimacy but also to ensure that its decisions match those that the community wishes to make for itself. The community can take informed decisions if the government makes sure that a full national debate takes place whenever major choices are to be made or policies decided. A number of submissions to the Commission from professional associations in the NHS have stressed their concern that patients need to be better informed about health issues. Even the vexed question of the high number of patients who do not keep hospital appointments turns out on examination to be more closely related to hospitals having a poor approach to patient relations, not reminding them of appointments after sometimes months of waiting, than to a lax attitude among the public. The issue derives from lack of accountability and the associated producer-oriented culture in hospitals rather than from a systemic propensity to miss appointments. 'Do Not Attends' (DNAs) do not undermine the case for making the NHS more accountable; rather they reinforce it.*

For their part, patients and potential patients in the form of the healthy citizen increasingly refuse to be treated as subjects of a paternalistic health service; they want a voice, influence over decisions that affect them, and redress for their grievances. They want the NHS to look out for their individual concerns. There is a growing temptation to turn to the courts and the language of human rights to fill the gap.

There is no doubt that the concept of individual rights has a valuable role to play in securing justice and fairness in particular cases in the National Health Service. There might well be occasions where the assertion of rights such as the right to life or to security of the person (both to be found in the recently enacted Human Rights Act) provide an important means to improve the quality of NHS provision for the general public. But it would be a mistake to see reliance on the courts and human rights as a substitute for thinking hard about issues of principle relating to the public interest, and to the proper accountability and therefore the legitimacy of the National Health Service. The assertion of individual rights through litigation is no substitute for voicing the public interest through collective decision-making rooted in democratic choices and thoroughly canvassed social preferences, and with built-in checks, balances and processes of accountability.

---

*See Jackson, S., 'Does organizational culture affect out-patient DNA rates?' *Health Manpower Management*, Bradford, 23(6), pp. 233–6, 1997. Also Burton, B., and Marlar, S., 'DNAs: cracking the code', *Health Director*, Dec./Jan. 4, p. 11, 1993.

3

THE DECLINE AND FALL OF NHS ACCOUNTABILITY

THE DEMOCRATIC DEFICIT within the NHS can be traced back to its inception. The 1948 NHS was built on a complex compromise that produced a tripartite structure in which democratic accountability was minimal. The hospital service was nationalised and made directly accountable to the Secretary of State through 14 regional hospital boards and boards of governors. General practitioners retained their independent contractor status, but again with administrative accountability to the Secretary of State through the same network of boards, all of whose members were appointed rather than elected. The only overt democratic input came via local authorities who retained control of 146 local health authorities responsible for services such as community nursing, midwifery, health visitors and school health clinics. Aneurin Bevan softened his earlier refusal to offer a democratic course by offering positions on boards to local councillors and trade union officials. He soon came to regret this democratic 'defect', saying that 'election is a better principle than selection'.

This structure survived until the 1974 reorganisation of the NHS when the democratic influence of local authorities was formally removed, although councillors still retained their seats on regional health boards. By 1968 local health authorities were managing nursing services, social services, the aftercare of the mentally ill or handicapped, ambulances and child and school health clinics. They needed to build health centres to accommodate their own staff, nurses, health visitors and dentists, and by renting space to family doctors the concept of an integrated health centre came closer to being realised. By 1974 15 per cent of GPs worked in such centres, with numbers rising at about 2.5 per cent per year – a notable increase in local authority influence over health. However, under the 1974 reorganisation this advance was halted. Community health services including health centres were removed from local authority control. Community Health Councils were introduced as local watchdogs, with local authorities and government appointees nominated to their boards. (See chapter 6 for more details).

Following the 1990 NHS and Community Care Act the last vestigial local authority representation was removed from regional and local boards. In a further radical reorganisation of the NHS, power was concentrated still more with the NHS Executive and Department of Health when in 1994 representative Regional Health Authorities were replaced by Regional Offices of the Executive. The 1991 NHS and Community Care Act also established hospitals and community health services as NHS trusts with appointed boards. NHS trusts are self-governing public corporations charged with the independent custodianship of the assets and revenues they manage. There was no longer any place for the tenuous links with local authorities that the involvement of council members had given the NHS; health authorities lost their obligation to accept local councillors and trade unionists. Instead chairmen are appointed by the Secretary of State, with the inevitable opportunity for political bias to operate.

With Regional Health Authorities now subsumed into the NHS Executive, leaving only a Regional Chairman in theory to represent the public view in high places, the independent public input diminished to vanishing point at that level as well. The National Consumer Council in its evidence to the Commission remarked that 'the role of the regional offices is not generally apparent to public view. Regional offices are outposts of the NHS Executive, and thus directly accountable upwards to the Secretary of State, but with no apparent 'downwards' accountability structure. They have many new responsibilities in the "new NHS", and it is not apparent how they will account for them to the public.'

The 1998 NHS Act increased the complexity of accountability arrangements, creating PCGs that will have shadow boards accountable to the health authorities and PCTs that again will have boards made up of political appointees but that will be autonomous independent organisations just as NHS trusts currently are.

The Secretary of State and her or his ministers are nominally in charge of all the major policy-making and decision-taking in the service. Below them at the Department of Health are two sets of important civil servants: one set are the departmental bureaucrats who are responsible for policy; the other set work under the NHS chief executive and are responsible for the day-to-day running of the service. In practice, of course, these formally separate functions merge into one another.

It is argued that there is a significant filament of accountability in these arrangements. The regional offices, health authorities, trusts and Primary Care Groups (PCGs), as well as a host of other public bodies, advisory committees, task forces and the like, are all ultimately responsible to the Health Secretary, who is answerable to Parliament for all their activities. She or he is also in theory responsible for the actions and decisions of all the officials who serve in the NHS, the department and their other public authorities and bodies. The Health Secretary and others come under parliamentary scrutiny through individual MPs, select committees, Parliamentary Questions, the Parliamentary Commissioner for Health, and public audit. (See Annex 2 for a description of the current NHS structure in England, Scotland, Wales and Northern Ireland.)

Parliamentary accountability has not worked in practice as it is meant to in theory. Actual experience of a variety of political crises, ministerial blunders and outright scandals has shown that ministers are very rarely held responsible for their own or their officials' mistakes. Indeed, there is now an emerging doctrine that ministers cannot really be held responsible for the administrative actions or mistakes of their officials, who in their turn are not held publicly responsible because they act officially in the minister's name and not in their own right. Further, in the British system parliamentary scrutiny of the Health Secretary and other ministers is inevitably compromised by the fact that the majority of MPs will necessarily belong to the governing party, and they have a primary duty of loyalty to their government and ministers. The idea that it is practically possible for a huge and varied organisation like the NHS to be held responsible through such a narrow route of accountability strains belief and is naïve about the way British politics works in practice. As the Royal College of General Practitioners say in their evidence: 'Governance of the health service can hardly be described as democratic . . . the assertion that the appointment of lay members to authorities mitigates against a democratic deficit seems to us somewhat spurious. Joint working between local [authorities] and health authorities will remain difficult while the former are democratically accountable and the latter remain immune.'

The absence of effective accountability upwards is accentuated by the democratic vacuum below. The operations of the NHS at local level have been governed by appointed bodies that are no more accountable for hosts of local policy and resource decisions to the local communities they seek to serve than they are to a remote Secretary of State above. Health authorities and trusts are divorced from the local authorities that provide social services essential to overall health care, and thus community and public health is not provided in a holistic way.

In 1974, Community Health Councils were set up to plug the democratic gap and fend off calls for elected health bodies locally (see chapter 5). They can perform a valuable role as watchdogs, but they are no substitute for collective decision-making that involves the public at local level. Since the mid-1990s, against the background of a more activist, concerned and critical public, health authorities and local NHS bodies and trusts have tried to compensate for the democratic deficit. They have experimented with new ways of consulting and involving the public in policy and resource decisions.

Citizens' juries, modelled on such bodies in Germany and the USA, are the most popular of these new mechanisms, but policy panels, focus groups, user surveys and so on have also been introduced. As the name indicates, citizens' juries are small groups of local people who are recruited by market-research techniques to debate specific policy or resources issues and to frame broad recommendations to the health authority, trust or local authority that has summoned them. These juries, too small to be properly representative, usually meet for several days to be briefed on the issue before them, to take expert evidence and come to their conclusions under the guidance of moderators. The idea is that they should reach informed decisions through deliberative debate, ideally adopting a community rather than individual perspective. Their recommendations are not binding on the commissioning bodies, but they are generally advised at least to respond to them.

Citizens' juries are often clearly valuable exercises in public consultation, but the dangers are equally clear. There is a temptation to cut corners on the means used to recruit members, and even professional sampling techniques can produce unrepresentative juries on such a small scale. There is the risk that authorities will manage the agenda or influence the evidence that juries hear. How often are such juries likely to be given the opportunity to discuss the usually unspoken resource constraints or rationing processes that lie behind the options before them? Even where authorities seek to avoid undue influence, or employ a strongly independent moderator, it is hard to ensure that the information supplied is genuinely neutral.

We welcome these exercises in 'direct democracy' – citizens' juries, focus groups, panels, policy forums, and similar means of consulting the public. At their best they are enlightened exercises in consultation and encourage a stronger bond between authorities and their publics. But they are not substitutes either for authentic democratic bodies locally or for informed watchdogs, like the CHCs, that can bring their accumulated experience to bear on the policies and decisions of health authorities and trusts – and, on occasion, of governments too. Indeed they are a substitute for the dwindling accountability now built into NHS structures. Since they are also expensive, they cannot form the basis for any kind of comprehensive public involvement in local policy-making or resource allocation; and if they were 'managed' or led astray, their conclusions could provide an inaccurate or misleading representation of public opinion that would be hard to detect.

Any system of accountability must aim to promote accountability to the whole population. Equality means that everyone's needs are assessed and met on an equitable basis, regardless of race, gender, disability, sexuality, age, class or other factors. In particular the Secretary of State for Health and the chief executive of the NHS have accepted that the health service both as an employer and service provider must provide a better deal for people from ethnic minority groups, and are taking action to achieve this. Ethnic minorities are well represented in the commissioning and delivery structures of the NHS: for example London's 20 per cent ethnic population is matched by 19.6 per cent of health authority and trust members coming from ethnic minority groups. It is imperative that this balance is maintained by Primary Care Groups and Trusts.

4

MONEY

PUBLIC SPENDING ON health as a percentage of GDP has risen from 2.7 per cent in 1948 to around 6.5 per cent today. Although this is almost at the bottom end of the European range, British health outcomes have been close to the average. Part of the reason for the comparitive success of the NHS has been the low transaction costs associated with centralised management, the fact that risk is pooled across the whole population, and the ability of the NHS to use its monopoly power to buy goods and services cheaply. Low wages and poor conditions for nurses and other health workers are one unwelcome consequence.

From the outset the NHS was afflicted by a crisis of expenditure. Ministers underestimated the volume of unmet need and the Treasury saw the NHS as wasteful and in-efficient. Every successive minister was obliged to consider and impose on the NHS various cash savings schemes that ranged from user charges to cuts in levels of spending and services. It is telling that the Treasury itself commissioned an independent inquiry into the excessive expenditure claims. But the Guillebaud Report, finally published in 1956, found that far from the NHS creating excessive demands on govern-ment expenditure, its current net cost to public funds had fallen from 3.75 per cent of GDP in 1949/50 to 3.24 per cent in 1953/4. The report also acknowledged that capital invest-ment had fallen significantly as a proportion of GDP.

This crisis in both revenue and capital expenditure con-tinued to haunt the NHS. For example, the Hospital plan that ended in the mid 1970s with the oil crisis resulted in only a third of projected new hospitals being built, with much of the stock nineteenth-century and earlier in origin. Capital expenditure has never recovered to 1976 levels. And yet there has been a continuing Treasury belief that there is surplus capacity in both the revenue budgets and the capital holdings of the NHS. Indeed it has insisted on the introduction of capital charges and annual efficiency savings in an attempt to extract these from what it still regards as a recalcitrant public sector.

The introduction of the 'internal market' in 1991 inflicted a major shock. Internal economies of scale were weakened and administrative costs increased substantially. A major objection to the experiment was the way the new contracting relationships between purchasers and providers led to a pronounced focus on costs at the expense of benefits. The rhetoric of markets continues to be used in justifying changes that are almost entirely cost-driven. This rhetoric is badly misleading. Nothing resembling a perfectly competitive market is on the table. Even if it were, economic efficiency would be achieved without regard to the need for equitable distribution of benefits that is at the heart of the NHS. Even on its own best terms the 'internal market' was an inappropriate mechanism for the health service.

An equally important objection is the inequities it introduced through allowing perverse incentives to operate. The introduction of GP fundholding allowed one group of payers to choose low-risk groups of patients, offloading higher-risk patients on health authorities. At another level competition between providers for scarce budgets compounded the continuing atmosphere of 'crisis management'.

The NHS is now facing increasing financial problems; a third of health authorities and trusts are in serious financial difficulties, and the cumulative deficit for 1998/99 is £541 million pounds.* (NHS trusts have a financial duty to break even, and so must clear these deficits and move towards break-even over the next three years. How they do so is of

---

*Audit Commission, *A Healthy Balance*. London: Audit Commission, 1999.

critical importance to the public, patients, clinical and non-clinical staff alike.

The financial problems of the NHS are compounded by a failure in public debate to distinguish properly between the value for money we receive from the NHS and the overall level of funding. Indeed, the government's reporting on funding issues is almost deliberately designed to be confusing. Virtually all NHS expenditure (98 per cent in 1999–2000) is funded out of general taxation and national insurance contributions. The only other important source of revenue is patient charges, yielding about 2 per cent of the total budget in recent years. But these simple facts about the funding of the health service are routinely disguised by the government counting as extra NHS spending income produced from land sales, recycled NHS debt, the 'modernisation fund' and the Private Finance Initiative.

There is thus a gap between government's presentation of expenditure plans and the actual flow of funding into the NHS from the taxpayer and charges. This leads to a crucial lack of transparency in the presentation of government spending plans. The Comprehensive Spending Review, for example, obscures the extent to which capital refunds (the recycling of internally generated resources) rather than new money contributes to the overall total NHS budget.

The new capital charging system that purports to introduce proper accounting for the use of capital has perversely introduced a distortion into the costing of NHS services, and thus into estimates of efficiency. We are told repeatedly by ministers that trusts should be obliged to meet 'the full cost of their capital', with no acknowledgement that the 'cost of capital', far from being an economic fact, is determined as a matter of policy by the Treasury.

The NHS budget is usually voted as separate capital and revenue instalments, but the government has changed the accounting rules and the methods of paying for capital. The introduction of capital charges in 1991, so that trusts now try to make 6 per cent return on their assets, disguises the way in which capital is now paid for. The object is to force more economic use of assets, and generate productivity savings, but the consequence has more typically been deterioration in the financial position of the trusts. How different trusts choose to respond to these financial pressures has never been properly discussed or opened up for democratic discussion.

Throughout the 1980s and 1990s capital investment for hospital and community health services fell, and it has not yet since returned to the levels of the early 1970s. The NHS now has a backlog in estate maintenance estimated at over £2.5 billion, and many of its hospitals are over a hundred years old. Although there is a major new hospital building programme worth cumulatively £2.1 billion, it is financed by the Private Finance Initiative, asset sales and unidentifiable redirections of cash to service private-sector debt.

Intriguingly, by 1998/9 the NHS's capital account was not merely self-financing through land, asset sales and capital returns; it was yielding a cash surplus. Thus the money to fund capital comes from internally generated savings from the NHS budget and not new capital. Capital projects are no longer explicitly related to earmarked funding streams, so it is impossible to see how far NHS funds are being allocated between revenue and capital expenditure, and difficult to describe the effect on the operating budgets – another major shortfall of accountability.

From the same revenue stream that is being used to fund capital investment under the PFI, the NHS is having to fund pay awards ahead of inflation and meet other financial pressures including new technologies, drugs and equipment. Trusts must also clear their cumulative deficits. It is not possible to gauge how far the planned increase in the revenue budget will meet these competing demands.

But the major consequence of the introduction of capital charging and imposition of external financing limits was to make trusts responsible for their own capital investment strategies. Local affordability was to be the key determinant of investment. In effect this was a return to pre-1948, when wealthy hospitals and areas could afford to invest and poor areas could not. Now capital investment in the NHS is largely determined by the wealth of local areas. Trusts can only invest if they have a rich legacy of land and buildings to liquidate to finance the deals. The problem is that capital investment is no longer predicated upon regional prioritisation but instead upon local affordability. Moreover, meeting the health-care needs has largely been omitted in the new planning process.

Spending and resource allocation within the NHS

The allocation of resources and budgets within the NHS is of critical concern, since it is the basis of both economic efficiency (value for money) and social equity. The Resource Allocation Working Party (RAWP) was responsible in the 1970s for the introduction of a funding formula based on needs. Controls over the workforce had attempted to ensure fairer distribution of clinical labour. Over the years the formulae have been refined in attempts to reflect the health-care needs of individual areas, and attempts have been made to level spending up or down accordingly. In 1991, RAWP has been modified and is technically known as a weighted capitation: i.e., the population of given health districts is adjusted for socio-demographic measures of need.

Funding to regions and health authorities are allocated through various capital and revenue budgets. Health authorities and Health Boards in Scotland, for example, currently administer three main revenue budgets: the largest, a budget for hospital and community health services (calculated from a partial population needs-based formula, see above); a budget for community prescribing (partially derived from a needs-based formula); and a general medical services budget to pay for health services (other than prescribing) supplied by general practitioners.

It is not always transparent how budgets are set and allocated and there is considerable flexibility both within and outside the resource allocation formulae. Health authorities have considerable autonomy over how they spend resources – but this autonomy is of course constrained and shaped by current demands on the budget, as well as national and local priorities.

Under the NHS and Community Care Act 1990, GP fund-holders received their budgets according to the size of the patient lists, unlike health authorities, which receive their budgets on the strength of serving the population within an entire geographic area. The inflation and deflation of patient numbers on GP lists proved to be a problem in allocating resources; another major difficulty was brokering a relationship between health authorities and GPs whose funding jurisdictions did not overlap but who shared the same patients. Moreover, GP fundholding broke up the principle of risk pooling and risk sharing across the population, even though the demand-led character of the previous system had meant that it too produced serious inequalities. In the early stages some health authorities did not have enough left over after meeting their commitments to GP fundholders to meet the needs of their remaining population or even to provide emergency services.

New Labour has sought to address the problem, but has only partially reversed the process. Its central initiative is the introduction of Primary Care Groups (PCGs) and Primary Care Trusts (PCTs). Their operations will involve budgets and spending determined by two very different systems of funding and accountability – those of independently contracted general practitioners and the health authorities. Some 480 PCGs will hold a unified budget covering the three previously separately identified budgets we outlined above, but which is cash-limited. With this they will purchase services for the health needs of practice lists of around 100,000 (ranging from a low of 50,000 to a high of 250,000) and decide how the funding is to be allocated between community health services, the acute hospital sector, primary care and public health priorities.

The difficulties the Commission is identifying in allocating resources transparently will be compounded. PCTs and PFI services, unlike NHS trusts, will have commercial freedom to manage their budgets and broaden their scope for income generation, and as commercial entities they will also have the freedom to restrict access to key commercial information. Although each PCG will have to publish an 'accountability agreement' that will be open for public scrutiny, it is not known what it will contain. Moreover, government guidance says public reporting of PCG finance should not be in any detail. Faced with cash-limited budgets, PCGs will initially try to manage budgets by controlling clinicians' referral and prescribing and treatment practice. PCGs will come under pressure to control referrals to hospitals and prescribing even where they are appropriate. GPs will come up for the first time against the same sorts of constraints that the hospital and community sector are facing. It is likely, just as now in the acute and community health trusts, that PCTs' primary managerial focus will be cost and value-for-money oriented rather than trading off benefits against costs.

In summary, the NHS has suffered since its foundation from continual underfunding that successive governments have sought to disguise. Budget holders have undergone continual pressure to squeeze more from less with little attempt to assess whether the public want them to suffer from such pressure or would make different decisions given the resources available. Equity has been subordinate to the desire to promote a narrow conception of efficiency. Accountability has been low in the priorities of ministers over successive rounds of reform, and the current structure now militates against improvements in accountability. If we are to take the government at its word in its professed desire to lead the NHS to a more rational system of organisation, it should begin to show more sensitivity to these issues. A start has been made with the increase in funding; but the next phase must be to begin restoring the accountability the NHS has lost.

5

COMPLAINTS AND REDRESS

We have described the top-down formal systems of accountability in chapter 3. We now examine the NHS system for complaints and individual redress, the regulation of the professions within the NHS, and the roles of Community Health Councils and the courts, all of which make a contribution towards accountability on behalf of individual patients and their families.

NHS complaints procedures

The current NHS complaints procedure, introduced in 1996, has been widely criticised for being incompetent, opaque, and ineffective in bringing about reforms in the service. These criticisms have come from, among others, the Select Committee on Health, the Health Ombudsman, community health councils and the research community.* Frank Dobson, the former Secretary of State, acknowledged that: 'The present system is really a bit of a shambles ... and at the end of it none of the people concerned is satisfied ...'†

In the Commission's view, a complaints procedure should provide individual justice and act as an instrument of accountability and control, through which wrongful conduct

---

*ACHCEW, *The NHS Complaints Procedure – ACHCEW's Memorandum to the Public Administration Committee*. London: ACHCEW, 1999.
†Select Committee on Health Report HC549-I 1998–99.

can be checked and services improved. The need to contribute towards accountability on behalf of individuals and their families has been heightened by NHS reforms which, as detailed above, have led over the past ten years to less supervision from the centre of health-care providers.

Health-care complaints are dealt with by four different types of agency: the NHS and private provider agencies; health authorities; the Health Service Ombudsman; and the regulatory agencies. In different ways, these agencies seek to distinguish major or systemic problems from low-level grumbles. Patients cannot complain to the Health Ombudsman until they have exhausted the NHS complaints procedures, so the NHS complaints system screens complaints and acts as 'gatekeeper' to Ombudsman review. Patients can complain directly to all other agencies. The NHS providers and authorities have gatekeeper staff, known as 'convenors', who identify which complaints should be subject to a more thorough review; and regulatory agencies for the professions have their own internal gatekeeping system, investigating only serious complaints.

The NHS complaints procedure has three stages and covers all NHS trusts, primary care groups and health authorities. They are all required to establish 'front-line' procedures for immediately investigating and resolving complaints: the so-called 'local resolution'. This first-stage process is supposed to provide a quick and informal response. Patients thereafter have no right to go on to the second stage – a hearing by an independent panel – and do so only if an NHS convenor agrees. The panels seek to settle complaints by agreement and to achieve conciliation. They have very limited powers, though a fair degree of leeway in how they conduct their affairs, and cannot call witnesses or evidence, cannot refer cases to the disciplinary process, and may not review decisions about policy. Even panels convened to review complaints against health authorities purchasing or 'rationing' decisions are limited to assessing whether decisions are reached in a proper and reasonable manner, and may not suggest alternative decisions. Finally, their recommendations are not binding. The Health Ombudsman sits at the apex of this process, acting as a mechanism of last resort for complainants dissatisfied with the outcome of the internal stages.

The volume of written complaints about the health service has been falling slowly since 1996. In England alone, the number of written complaints received about Hospital and Community Health Services decreased by 3 per cent to 86,013 between 1997–98 and 1998–99, an overall decrease of some 8 per cent since the implementation of the complaints procedure in April 1996. Nearly two-thirds of these were dealt with within four weeks. In 1,838 cases the complainant requested an independent review, but only 285 (15 per cent) were allowed to go before a panel. Of these, 176 (60 per cent) were dealt with by the end of the year and 109 were still outstanding.

For the same period, the number of written complaints received about general medical and dental services and Family Health services administration rose by 2 per cent to 38,857. In 1,430 cases the complainant requested an independent review of their complaint, but only 313 (22 per cent) were referred to an independent review panel. Of these, 87 (28 per cent) were still being pursued at the end of the year.

The NHS complaints procedure was designed to act as a key mechanism for making the NHS more responsive to patient concerns and pre-defined standards. The complaints are regarded almost solely as information about defects in the system and are valued mainly for their contribution to raising standards. On this view, the purpose of complaints procedures is neither to provide individual justice nor to hold providers to account, but simply to inform organisational learning. They seem to have failed even in this limited aim.

Complainants do not believe that the procedures are fair or independent, and their informality reinforces this belief. The Select Committee for Public Administration commented in 1999 that the procedures required 'a strong element of formality' in order to ensure that they were seen as fair and impartial and commanded respect.* The ethos of informal

---

*Select Committee on Public Administration Report UC54 1998–99, Report of Health Service Ombudsman 1997–98.

resolution has rendered the first stage opaque to external scrutiny, and the crucial gatekeeping role of the convenor has proved to be highly unsatisfactory. In reviewing 117 cases of complaints against convenors, the Ombudsman identified a multitude of failings in their conduct, and their independence is fatally undermined by their position as non-executives on NHS trusts or health authorities.

A recent study by the Public Law Project found the thoroughness and competence of panel investigations to be seriously wanting.* The fact that the parties often do not meet has undermined complainants' confidence about the fairness of the procedures. The system is therefore a poor instrument of individual justice. Indeed, complainants often give up or are deterred from pursuing their complaints, and have limited rights of appeal. The evidence from AIMS (Association for Improvements in the Maternity Services) to the Commission complained about the variable quality of the meetings that complainants are offered, with key staff absent or inadequately briefed, so that the meetings often waste their time. 'Sometimes complainants who go to these meetings emerge more distressed and angrier than they were before.' Financial compensation for any hardship suffered is extremely rare.

The system is also a very weak instrument of accountability. If panel decisions are not enforced, sanctions or penalties cannot be applied and no compensation is provided. Nor does the complaints system provide controls on the behaviour of an NHS body or individual staff, and NHS managers rarely have to confront the failings that complaints might highlight. Overall it is not surprising that NHS complaints procedures have largely failed to bring about reforms of the service.

Existing arrangements also offer less control over GPs. Before 1996, complaints against GPs in primary care were handled by formal Medical Services Committees that provided an uncomfortable mixture of grievance-handling and a

---

*Wallace, H. and Mulcahy, L., *Cause for Complaint? An Evaluation of the Effectiveness of the NHS Complaints Procedure*. London: Public Law Project, 1999.

way of holding GPs to account. Now complainants are obliged to try and resolve problems with the GP or person they are complaining about, and the committees have a very marginal role in dealing with complaints.

The Health Service Commissioner (Ombudsman)

The Health Ombudsman is an officer of Parliament. The problems with the NHS complaints procedures provide something of an acid test of his influence. Complaints are clearly central to his expertise, and the operation of the NHS procedures strongly affects his work. But there are few signs that governments respond to his or Select Committee criticisms.

The Health Ombudsman's powers and role differ from those of the Parliamentary Ombudsman. He can investigate complaints about failures in service as well as mal-administration and clinical issues (this covers a wide range of topics, such as rudeness, unwillingness to treat a patient as a person with rights, refusal to answer reasonable questions, knowingly giving misleading or inadequate advice, partiality, offering no redress, ignoring valid advice, and so on). Although ostensibly concerned with individual justice, the Ombudsman service does inquire into and report on systemic problems. Much depends on his views and attitude. The current Ombudsman emphasises the individual justice aspects of his role. His jurisdiction includes NHS bodies, such as regional offices, health authorities and NHS trusts, as well as complaints arising from arrangements between health service and outside bodies (e.g., private clinics that provide services for NHS patients), NHS contracts and purchasing decisions, family health services including GPs' surgeries, and matters of clinical judgement.

Dealings involving private providers are something of a grey area for the Heath Ombudsman, as other Ombudsmen are precluded from investigating commercial transactions. Such transactions are not subject to judicial review and the courts are reluctant to interfere with government contractual arrangements, seeing them as private matters outside the remit of public law.* Official discussions about including such services and private health care have begun, and are so far unresolved. But this is an important issue, especially for people in long-term care who are paying their own way and cannot use the NHS complaints procedures.

There are important limits on the Ombudsman's remit. A time limit of one year applies. Not only must complainants exhaust the NHS procedures, but he can only consider a complaint if no legal remedy is available (which means that a complainant who cannot afford to pursue a justifiable case through the courts has no remedy at all). While he can investigate the merits of a clinical decision, he cannot consider the merits of an administrative or policy decision; and he has no powers to investigate the Department of Health or NHS executive. In practice, NHS complaints tend to be rejected because the NHS procedures are not exhausted. In 1998–99, broadly half the complaints to the Health Ombudsman were rejected as 'premature' – i.e., taken out before NHS procedures were exhausted. In all, the Ombudsman investigated only 157 complaints – a derisory total in a service that covers 56 million people, of whom some 125,000 complained in writing to the NHS last year. If individual justice is the aim, it is for the few. Financial compensation in hardship cases is even rarer – only five cases in 1998–99.

The Health Ombudsman can only recommend what redress seems to him to be appropriate, and cannot enforce any course of action. The main sanction is to 'name and shame' individual health-care professionals, health authorities or trusts by reporting in some detail on their behaviour: a fairly rare occurrence. His annual reports are reviewed by the Select Committee on Public Administration, which may call witnesses, ask questions and make recommendations to the Secretary of State. The committee is forthright in its criticism of individual chairs of health authorities, chief executives and clinicians. In very serious cases, it calls for an individual's resignation, but has no powers to bring this about. When

---

*Drewry, G., and Oliver, D., *Public Service Reforms – Issues of Accountability and Public Law*. Pinter, 1996.

complaints about particular problems recur, the committee usually draws specific conclusions and makes policy recommendations. But while they have been making such recommendations almost every year since 1976, the Ombudsman's inquiries year after year reveal the same failings!

The Health Committee wanted the Ombudsman to review whether his recommendations were being implemented, but he responded that he had neither the statutory powers nor the resources to conduct a continuing management audit of the NHS. Even though the Department of Health issues guidance in response to Ombudsman reports, all too often such guidance already exists but is not being followed.

Worse still, the outgoing NHS chief executive, Alan Langlands, giving evidence to the committee in 1998, appeared at a loss to suggest how the NHS might be controlled. He expressed doubt about how far the NHS Executive itself could monitor an organisation the size of the Health Service in detail. Admittedly, then he was talking about an NHS that relied heavily upon contractual relationships within the internal market and his regional offices were required to adopt 'a hands-off approach', only intervening in extreme cases. But the contractual approach remains in place; and as the committee pointed out, contractual arrangements often fail patients and are too loosely framed to be used as effective tools 'for ensuring that good quality care [is] provided'.*

The select committee has twice recently reviewed the NHS complaints procedures, on both occasions commenting on the failures of convenors, and additionally (in 1998–99) criticising the lack of monitoring of independent review panels, reaffirming the need for independence, and arguing for more formal procedures to ensure that they commanded public respect and were seen as fair and impartial. But the government rejected its advice, arguing that 'the degree of formality' did not prejudice complainants' perceptions of the system. Rather than accept the Ombudsman's findings in

*Select Committee on Public Administration Second Report, Report of the Health Services Commissioner 1996–7, HC352.

numerous reports and the conclusions of two select committee deliberations, the then Health Secretary chose to wait upon a department-funded evaluation.

The committee has also recommended changes to give panels more powers, to summon witnesses and take evidence, to hold clinicians, trusts and authorities to account, and to recommend disciplinary action. It has raised concerns about the impartiality of the procedures, and proposed that panel members should not be connected with the trust or authority subject to complaint; that panels should accountable to the NHS Executive's regional offices that trusts and health authorities should be required to make a formal response to panel findings; and that any major concerns should be reported to the Commission for Health Improvement. There is no response as yet from the government.

Private health care

The rules governing complaints procedures in the private sector are patchy. Neither nursing homes nor private hospitals are obliged to run complaints procedures. Infertility clinics are required to have a complaints procedure for registration with the Human Fertilisation and Embryology Authority. People complaining about private care services funded by the NHS (e.g., nursing home residents) can complain to the NHS authority or trust under the NHS complaints procedure. But the NHS authority that has commissioned the privately run home or clinic may have a conflict of interest in dealing with such complaints. For example, it may not wish to raise a complaint if the provider is otherwise performing satisfactorily, even if the complaint means a lot to the complainant. Complaints may expose issues where the contract is not clear or where there is a dispute between the NHS and the provider. There is considerable potential for buck-passing between the NHS authority commissioning the provider and the provider.

The main route of complaint for private patients is to the relevant professional or registration agency. But a Health Select Committee review in 1999 noted that these regulators often do not adequately handle such complaints.* The committee recommended more effective and consistent enforcement of the existing legislation, but it is not the primary function of these agencies to handle disputes between patients and providers. The committee recommended stronger mandatory procedures, with independent review by a separate Health Ombudsman for the independent sector. The Care Standards Bill 1999 proposes a mandatory internal procedure for private providers, but fails to stipulate arrangements for independent review or (as yet) for external review by an independent sector Ombudsman.

Professional regulation

Most health workers are bound by rules governing standards of care and ethical conduct drawn up by two main self-regulating professional associations: the General Medical Council (GMC) for doctors and the United Kingdom Central Council for Nursing, Midwifery and Health Visiting (UKCC). They are charged to protect the public interest and operate under licence granted by Act of Parliament. Generally, the Acts that establish the GMC, UKCC and other self-regulatory professional agencies overseeing health disciplines have a common form. A practitioner who registers with the GMC, or another regulatory body, must fulfil conditions laid down by the regulatory agency to ensure his or her fitness for practice. The agency's main sanction is to remove a practitioner from the relevant register or to remove the facilities licence – a draconian measure that is therefore seldom applied.

The GMC, as it acknowledged in its evidence to the Commission, is not concerned with systemic issues (e.g., resource allocation, rationing, staffing levels) as causes of medical mishap, or with how effectively current complaints procedures operate. Its interest in complaints is rather in the

---

*Select Committee on Health Fifth Report HC281 1 1998–9, *The Regulation of Private and Other Independent Health Care*. London: The Stationery Office.

information they provide about whether registered practitioners keep to the terms of their registration and are thus fit to practise. This can be their only interest in complaints, as they do not have a legal mandate for resolving or adjudicating on general disputes between patients and providers, however significant they may be. The weakness of their powers has been cruelly exposed by the case of the Bristol heart operations on babies and the convictions for murder of Dr Harold Shipman.

More generally, the GMC has traditionally relied solely on complaints from the public to trigger investigations into the behaviour of doctors. Like the UKCC and other self-regulating agencies that license health-care practitioners, the GMC has acted only if a complaint indicates that there might be a breach of the GMC rules. In recent years, the GMC criteria for 'fitness to practise' have broadened in scope with the introduction of procedures for investigation of doctors whose health appears to be failing and whose competence is questioned. Nevertheless the Council has no mandate for dealing with complaints between doctors and their patients in general.

A recent *Which?* survey found that four out of five people who complained to the GMC were dissatisfied with the fairness of the process.* Very few complaints result in some kind of action being taken against the doctor: in the *Which?* survey, only six out of 284 cases inspired action; more generally, only 45 out of 2,500 complaints to the GMC in 1997 were considered serious enough to be heard and adjudicated upon by the Professional Conduct Committee. Yet only about one in four people who complain want the doctor struck off; most simply want formal recognition that a mistake has occurred, or seek to prevent the same thing happening again.

Such inadequacies were exposed in the recent Shipman and Bristol cases. The GMC is not empowered to initiate investigations, to monitor good practice by regular scrutiny

---

*'The GMC: Working for Patients?', *Health Which?*, October 1999, pp. 18–22.

and audit, or to apply sanctions in cases of bad practice. Rather it acts only as the disciplinary body for the medical profession once a problem has been exposed. The GMC has begun over the past five years to improve its procedures for promoting best practice and increasing lay representation, and is developing a system of re-validation for doctors (with backing from the British Medical Association and the Royal Colleges). The Commission recommends that such moves must increase its capacity to act decisively when cases demand it; and re-validation must involve patients and lay persons in the regular examination of doctors' delivery of health care, and their professional expertise (and training) and competence.

The UKCC sees the primary purpose of regulation as to protect the safety of the public, and so involves the public in its work. A third of its governing council are user represent-atives, albeit nominated by the Secretary of State; and the UKCC has an officer for consumer affairs and a consumer involvement strategy. The Commission was impressed by the UKCC's commitment to promote lay involvement and extend best practice, although, like the GMC, its capacity for proactive intervention is limited. The Royal Colleges are responsible for the professional standards and training of specialist doctors and surgeons (though the Royal College of General Practitioners is responsible for GP training). They are autonomous and influential organisations, accountable to their own members and fellows, that act as powerful advocates of their members' interests. They possess even fewer powers over their members than the GMC and UKCC and involve fewer lay persons. There is, for example, no discernible public input into their regulation or professional training.

There is now a growing trend of legislation imposing wider responsibilities on all NHS regulatory bodies and introducing lay representation into their governing processes – a movement reflected in the recommendations of this report. But this applies only to those with powers over health-care professions, and the regulators for private providers are exempt.

Community Health Councils

Government set up Community Health Councils (CHCs) in 1974 as champions of the patient at local level, following scandals in some long-term-care hospitals and the removal of health centres from local authority control. Their role was to assert the public interest in health to health authorities at local level – an option the government preferred both to elected health authorities and to local authority control of any part of the NHS. There are 206 CHCs in England and Wales. They have an over-arching national organisation, the Association of Community Health Councils of England and Wales (ACHCEW). In Scotland, sixteen Local Health Councils perform equivalent functions, and Northern Ireland has four Health and Social Services Boards which are in effect local quangos. Every health authority in England and Wales has a statutory obligation to have a CHC as its watchdog. CHC membership is voluntary and unpaid. Half the members are nominated by local authorities; a third are elected by voluntary organisations from among their members; and a sixth are appointed by the Secretary of State.

CHC members have the right to visit NHS premises at any time of day or night, and health authorities and trusts are obliged to respond to their reports. They have a right to be consulted on any substantial variations in service provision. They advise health authorities on what they consider to be the impact of their decisions and any objections to those decisions must be referred through the NHS Executive's regional offices to the Secretary of State for adjudication. (In the case of Welsh CHCs, objections have been channelled through the Welsh Office.) CHCs in Wales have recently been reorganised into a range of federal models, although their statutory remit remains unchanged.

But since they were first set up, CHCs have laboured under difficulties, some of them inherent in the system, some of their own making, some because the legislation imposed on them from above has failed to keep pace with the changes governments have introduced into the NHS. Not all those in authority have recognised their potential – or if they have, they have in some cases been alarmed by it or have resisted it. Despite their statutory status, CHCs are unincorporated bodies, and so their members have no legal indemnity. If they mount a legal challenge to a health authority and lose, which is always possible even with an apparently cast-iron case, their members are jointly and severally responsible for any costs incurred – a crippling handicap.

The right to be consulted on substantial variations in service is enshrined in legislation, but has diminished in value over the years because no practical definition of the word 'substantial' has ever been forthcoming. In 1985 John Patten, then a Parliamentary Undersecretary of State for Health, informed an MP that he would expect health authorities to 'go along with a CHC's views in most cases'.* He pointed out that CHCs could refer any case they were unhappy about to a regional health authority, now of course abolished. Latterly, health authorities have taken unto themselves to determine which of their decisions are 'substantial', and have consulted, or not consulted, on that basis.

While CHCs can refer disputed decisions to Whitehall for adjudication by the Secretary of State, the process is time-consuming and opaque. CHCs do not see, for example, the representations made by NHS officers in any disputed referral. When rulings are made, it is not clear why.

The arrangements for recruiting members means that members vary a great deal in their availability and commitment and may have differing and sometimes conflicting personal and organisational agendas. The local authority nominees, if they are councillors (which they do not have to be), are very busy people who cannot always give the necessary time to CHC duties. Larger voluntary organisations, which may have several branches in any one area, are sometimes over-represented through the elective process. There is also a tendency for the successful candidates to concentrate on their own special interests rather than on the wider picture. The Secretary of State's nominees are felt to be imposed from above rather than being appointed with

---

*Letter to Jeff Rooker MP, 5 February 1985.

57

due attention to the need for representative local appointments.

On the other hand, local authority nominees are seen as the only true democratic input into CHCs. Voluntary organisations are also close to the people and in touch with users of NHS services. In some regions, CHCs nominate and help select the Secretary of State's appointees; this section is therefore valued as one over which the CHCs themselves have an influence, and selection procedures can be fairly rigorous.

Because CHCs are autonomous bodies, standards vary across the country. CHCs are not accountable for the way they take decisions. Reviews and performance appraisal are variable. Training is not mandatory and outcomes are not routinely monitored nor assessed. This lack of consistency is exacerbated by the awkward establishing arrangements for CHCs. The NHS Executive's regional offices are their establishing authorities, and the eight regional offices across the country each have different ideas as to how CHCs should be managed.

The position of ACHCEW, itself a statutory body, is difficult and anomalous. It largely depends for its funding on contributing CHCs, whose membership, being voluntary, can be withdrawn, thus creating instability. ACHCEW has no power to require good standards to be maintained. It can only try to persuade, by spreading information on best practice. This can easily be ignored.

The already very limited statutory rights of CHCs have been eroded over the past decade by changes in the NHS which, as pointed out above, have not been matched by changes in legislation affecting CHCs. For example, they now have to negotiate a visiting and monitoring brief in respect of the residential and nursing homes that have replaced the long-stay hospitals over which they previously had statutory visiting and monitoring rights. They do not always succeed in gaining entry. Much recuperative and rehabilitative work which at one time was carried out in acute hospitals is now done in patients' homes and cannot be independently monitored. CHCs have traditionally had observer status with speaking rights at health authority meetings, but they have no such status, as of right, on the new commissioning Primary Care Groups, soon to be trusts.

Given all this confusion and obfuscation, it is perhaps not surprising that among CHCs in general and within individual CHCs there exists some ambivalence over their ethos and role. Some CHC members, and some CHCs, appear to see themselves as the public relations arm of health authorities, whose function is to reconcile the public to the inevitability of the authorities' plans and proposals, particularly with regard to economies and cuts in services. This is very comfortable for health authorities and regional offices, and disposes some of them to view those CHCs that try to play a challenging 'watchdog' role as churlish, confrontational, oppositional – and dispensable.

In 1991, health authorities proclaimed that they were thenceforward to be regarded as 'champions of the people'. The challenge to CHCs was obvious, especially as the role of CHCs was neglected in the 1991 reforms. While health authorities quite properly experimented with new ways of consulting the public – through citizens' juries, focus groups, panels, etc, as described in chapter 3 – and should be commended for doing so, they sometimes seemed to be motivated by a desire to undermine and marginalise CHCs.

Yet CHCs still survive, and their worth and potential has been more explicitly recognised recently than ever before. A recent CSV report found that it would cost nearly £8 million to provide an equivalent service with paid rather than voluntary members.* Frank Dobson, the then Health Secretary, said at the 1998 ACHCEW conference:

I look to Community Health Councils to continue to play a role in ensuring that the patient's and public's views are known to the NHS decision-makers both nationally and locally . . . As I see it, this is the focus of your role and it is for you to fulfil it in the most effective way you can to assist in developing better and more widespread public involve-

*Hidden Volunteer, January 2000, Community Service Volunteers (CSV).

59

ment in the development of NHS services . . . Go on doing what you're doing now, but do it better!

The recently formed Parliamentary Group on Community Health Councils has 240 MPs and is one of the largest in Parliament. Its establishment has given a fillip to the cause of strengthening and resourcing reformed CHCs.

The law

The courts can provide a last-resort mechanism of redress and a form of accountability. Litigation involving health authorities and hospitals has assumed a higher profile in recent years, and though actual cases of judicial review of government decisions seemed to number no more than an average of about a dozen annually in the mid-1990s, cases involving the NHS as a whole seem now to be on the increase.* The rise in disciplinary proceedings in relation to the medical and other health-related professions seems to have brought about a growing recourse to the courts. These cases seek to engage the law in overseeing what have long been considered the managerial prerogatives of the NHS, such as the allocating of resources and authorising of new medical treatments and pharmaceutical products.

Negligence actions against doctors and hospitals and other branches of the health service have multiplied. The implementation of the Human Rights Act 1998 on 2 October 2000 is likely to produce a new burst of litigation, with individuals seeking to achieve their health goals by characterising their desires as judicially enforceable human rights under the new legislation.

It is of course appropriate for individuals to rely on the law to defend themselves from unlawful action by branches of the health service, just as it is right for them to seek to use the law either to secure the right treatment from their health authority or to win damages to compensate them for having been treated

---

*Weir, S., and Beetham, D., *Political Power and Democratic Control in Britain*, Table 15.1, Routledge, 1999.

badly. Each and every such case must be considered separately and viewed on its own merits. It is wrong to castigate the law for having so greatly increased its involvement in the health service in recent years. And it is also wrong to blame individuals and others for turning to the law to further their interests within the health service. The weaknesses of the complaints procedures, described above, no doubt drive them to more effective remedies. The negligence action, for example, has been one of the few truly effective ways in which users of the service have been able to achieve adequate and effective accountability for tragic wrongs that they feel have been done to them or their family within the NHS.

We have received clear evidence to the effect that for many claimants such negligence actions have often been a last-gasp initiative, turned to only after a succession of failures to achieve redress elsewhere. Likewise, many judicial review applications have been born out of a desperate sense of hopelessness and out of an inability effectively to penetrate the secrecy with which NHS decisions are currently enshrouded. Such judicial review cases have not infrequently secured real gains of lasting value to patients. And they have often been the only route through which to elicit the kind of information and data from the NHS that we believe should be available by right.

Even a properly functioning health service will attract, possibly frequently, the involvement of the law. All public authorities in the land must adhere to the principles of legality. This is why we recognise that the courts should ultimately have the residual power as a matter of law to protect the NHS constitution that we propose in the Executive Summary, and later in chapter 7, from being subverted or ignored by the institutions that are supposed to be its servants. In the same way, the criminal law provides an important and at times essential forum for punishing severe wrongs done by members of the health service, whether they be doctors, nurses, or (even) managers. The recently concluded trial of Dr Harold Shipman is a stark illustration of this fact. Likewise we accept that some system of compensation for damage done to individuals by the health service will continue to be required, though whether in the form of the present action for negligence or through some other system based on strict liability is beyond the scope of this report to discuss.

What matters is not the principle of the availability of such recourses to law, but the context in which such litigation occurs. At present the perceived secrecy of the NHS and the lack of proper accountability in the system as a whole leads to an over-reliance on law as a means of achieving the responses and the transparency that should be a matter of right. The heavy involvement of the law in a public service is a measure of its failure rather than its success. We are confident that a properly functioning and democratically accountable health service would be one in which the law would be a tool of last resort to be used reluctantly, rather than the first stop for the (rightly or wrongly) disgruntled that it so often is today.

The point made above is clearest of all in relation to the Human Rights Act. There is no explicit guarantee of adequate health treatment in the legislation, but there are other rights (e.g., to life, to protection from cruel, inhuman and degrading treatment, and to privacy) that we are certain will underpin many novel legal actions against health authorities and other health bodies. Particularly important in this regard is likely to be Article 14 of the European Convention, which prohibits unjustifiable discrimination in the enjoyment of other Convention rights. We are clear that in many instances such litigation can be expected to produce outcomes that will not only be welcome to the people taking the actions but that may also produce a net benefit to the health service as a whole.

Valuable though rights litigation is certain to be in individual cases, it is not the appropriate mechanism through which to meet the demands for participation, transparency and accountability that are now laid quite properly on the health service as a whole. Like the law in general, the Human Rights Act will provide an important fall-back opportunity for individuals whom the system has grievously failed. Accordingly it will work most efficiently for the public interest as a whole in the context of a reformed NHS that has met and dealt with many of the grievances and complaints that currently surround the system and which – in the absence of reform – would be expected to precipitate yet more increases in litigation.

Voluntary organisations

Certain voluntary organisations act as advocates and campaigners for patients and particular groups of patients (e.g., those that campaign for improved mental health services). We welcome their contribution to debates about health care and the priorities of the health service, just as we acknowledge the contribution that they and other voluntary groups often make as funders (e.g., of cancer research) and as providers of health care (e.g., of HIV/AIDS services). As non-NHS providers of health care, voluntary organisations are technically accountable to the health authorities with which they have contracts to deliver specified services, but most would also see themselves as primarily accountable to their service users. Voluntary organisations can assist in opening up NHS institutions and decisions to informed public scrutiny, and in illuminating the need to pay attention to neglected patients and people suffering from particular conditions or illnesses. But voluntary organisations are in no sense a substitute for proper procedures for dealing with complaints or providing redress, or for democratic channels of accountability within the service itself.

6

PRACTICE IN EUROPE

THROUGHOUT THIS REPORT we have shown that the NHS is not publicly accountable. In considering reforms to make the service more open, accountable and democratic, we have looked briefly at the experiences of other countries, especially in Europe. In particular, we have taken as a guide the views and recommendations of the Council of Europe. Clearly, European states vary a great deal in the way their health services are organised and delivered, and we were not seeking an existing system on which to model a reformed NHS. One of our key principles is that we must build on what we have got in the United Kingdom, and as far as possible in an evolutionary way. Thus, while we take the view that no one system of organisation and delivery could provide the answers to the current problems of accountability in the NHS, there are principles and areas of good practice from which the NHS could learn.

Our starting point is the latest set of guidelines to member states of the Council of Europe's Committee of Ministers on developing structures for citizen and patient participation in decision-making processes on health care (Recommendation No. R (2000) 5 of the Committee of Ministers, 24 February 2000; see Annex 3 for fuller detail). The Committee's main recommendation is that the governments of member states, including the United Kingdom, should ensure that all citizens are able to participate in all areas of decision-making in their country's health-care systems, at national, regional and local levels; and that the principle of participation 'in all aspects' of health care should be observed by all health-care authorities, managers, professionals, insurers and all other 'operators'. The Committee further recommends that member states should create legal structures and policies promoting citizens' participation and patients' rights in their health-care systems, reflecting the Council of Europe's guidelines; and that they should adopt policies to encourage and support the growth of voluntary organisations of health-care users.

In the Committee's view, the goals of citizen participation and empowerment of patients can be achieved only if basic patients' rights are implemented and patient participation, in its turn, is a means to ensure that these basic rights are observed in daily practice. The Committee sets out differing levels of participation, ranging from influence on the overall administration of the health-care system and on the decision-making process to furthering particular interests through organisations of patients or citizens; elected or user representation on boards or executive bodies governing health-care bodies; and direct influence over the provision of health care through individuals' freedom of choice.

The proposals we make for democratising the NHS reflect this expression of the latest thinking in Europe. In particular, our proposal that the government should draw up a constitution for the NHS in consultation with the public fits squarely, in principle, practice and spirit, with the Committee's recommendation that European states should create legal structures and policies that promote citizens' participation and patients' rights in their health-care systems. Our proposals for elected health authorities and patient and lay representation on NHS trusts and Primary Care Groups would provide a strong structural setting for improved citizen participation; and our proposals for strengthening community health councils mesh with the Council of Europe's desire to create voluntary movements of user organisations throughout Europe. In our brief survey of European practice, we found interesting examples of the practical participation of users in providing services, and we would like to see more experiments on such lines in this country.

We were greatly encouraged by the emphasis that the

Council of Europe gave to the idea of a participatory democracy in the explanation of the Committee's proposals. For example, the Committee stresses that citizens in a democracy should 'determine the goals and targets of the health-care sector'; that the system should be 'patient-oriented'; and that 'citizens should *necessarily* [our emphasis] participate in decisions regarding their health care'. The Committee further recognised the important role that civic and self-help organisations of patients, consumers, insured persons and citizens should play in representing 'users'' interests in health care and in providing support and services in their members' interests. Like the Commission, the Committee believes that a participatory health-care system will help to broaden the public's general knowledge about health problems, and that taking part in decision-making processes will lead to public acceptance of health policy goals. Further, its members assume that it will assist countries to promote healthy living and disease prevention, encourage citizens to take responsibility for their own health, and generally 're-vitalise representative democracy' and 'enhance social cohesion' as well as lead to a more effective health-care system and a better balance of interests among the various players and interest groups involved.

We give pride of place to the recommendations of the Committee of Ministers, but there is a host of international and European instruments and conventions that stress the value of participatory democracy and citizen and patient involvement in health-care systems. Some are clear precedents for the Committee of Ministers' new round of proposals for democracy in health care, beginning with the European Social Charter (Article 11) on the right to the protection of health. The Convention on Human Rights and Biomedicine requires signatory states to provide '*equitable access* [our emphasis] to health care of appropriate quality' (Article 3) and a right for all citizens to information about their health (Article 10). The World Health Organisation's Health 21 programme for the European region and recent WHO policy documents make recommendations for patients' rights and citizens' participation. Further, the Amsterdam Declaration on the

Promotion of Patients' Rights in Europe stresses the need for health-care systems that focus on people and allow the 'citizen's voice and choice to influence the way in which health services are designed and operate', and outside Europe the Ottawa Charter for Health Promotion (1986) and the Jakarta Declaration on Leading Health Promotion into the 21st Century (1997) are significant statements on the guiding principles for citizen participation in public health.

Countries throughout Europe have sought to develop patients' rights. The World Health Organisation considers that certain benefits follow such advances. Patients are put on more equal terms with doctors and other providers within a closer 'democratic communication'; there is more emphasis on the quality of care; patients' rights to information about their condition and treatment and their choice of provider are acknowledged; and patients' organisations have greater opportunities to influence principles and priorities of care, its protocols and processes.

Patients' rights are sometimes enshrined in legislation rather than in a code, or charter, as in the United Kingdom. As a result, individual citizens can turn to the courts if their patient's rights have been breached. In the Netherlands, the Medical Contracts Act (1995) is intended to 'strengthen the legal position' of patients by clarifying their rights in relation to health care.* Under this act, patients have the right, for example, to choose a general practitioner, and to be given information about proposed examinations. Some countries, such as Norway, are using charters, alongside legal avenues, to strengthen patients' rights. Although charters generally refer to 'rights', the provisions of the charters, as in the UK, are not legally binding.

The Commission is sympathetic to the overwhelming public view that a British Bill of Rights should include a right to 'free medical treatment at the time of need'. But we would not wish to see the individual rights of patients

---

*World Health Organisation Regional Office for Europe, *European Health Care Reforms, Citizens' Choice and Patients' Rights*. Copenhagen: WHO Regional Office for Europe, 1996.

develop in the UK in such a way that only through the courts could the public exert influence over health policies and priorities or gain redress. Upholding the legally entrenched rights of individuals or commercial organisations does not always accord with the best interests of the wider public. For this reason we choose to promote patients' rights by means of an improved Patients' Charter alongside an effective complaints process and within a genuinely participatory health-care system that allows citizens and patients to make democratic choices and secures accountability in an equitable and collective manner.

Complaints are a useful tool for helping the NHS to learn from mistakes and drive up standards as well as giving individual patients quick and effective redress where justified. Yet, as we argued in chapter 5, the NHS complaints process is far from satisfactory. In particular, complainants question the lack of independence in its procedures. For these reasons we recommend that independent review panels should handle all complaints. In the Netherlands, patients who object to the way their complaints are handled can by law appeal to an independent regional committee. In Iceland, disputes can be referred to an independent committee of three people appointed by the Minister of Health after nomination by the Supreme Court. Committee members cannot be employed by the health-care service. In Finland, every health-care institution must by law have a patient ombudsman. The role of the ombudsmen includes providing information about patients' rights and assisting individuals with complaints.

One of the Commission's recommendations is that Community Health Councils be given a formal constitutional role to act as patients' watchdogs and as advocates for those who wish to pursue a complaint. The Council of Europe's emphasis on the role of user and voluntary organisations, together with provision in Europe for health services run by employee and user boards, provides principled and practical support for our recommendation. Day-to-day experience in Europe shows that strong patients' groups can offer the opportunity to influence the organisation and provision of health care or even to provide it directly. One authoritative team of observers notes the argument that 'taking the views and opinions of citizens into account, through increased participation in the policy-making or decision-making process, for example, may serve as a means of democratising health services, thus making the medical profession and the state more accountable'.*

In our view, strengthening CHCs would help to achieve these and other wider aims. In Italy, the Tribunal for Patients' Rights (the Tribunal) has developed alongside the state-run health service and has become an extremely effective vehicle for citizens' voices. There are similarities between CHCs and the Tribunal. 'The Tribunal for Patients' Rights is a network of nuclei, comprised of ordinary citizens, volunteering their efforts and experience to monitoring the quality of health services, collecting and resolving patients' complaints . . . Nuclei of the Tribunal are regularly present in every community health unit, in every major health structure, throughout the nation. They answer to a Regional Secretary of the Federation Democratic Movement who offers organisational resources, references and co-ordination'.†

The Commission also argues vigorously for integrating democracy through elections in the running of the NHS. Various European countries devolve responsibility for running their health service to elected bodies, usually at regional level, or share that responsibility between central government and elected regional and local authorities. In this sense, our proposals that control of the NHS should no longer be the exclusive responsibility of central government, but rather shared between the centre and elected bodies at regional and local level, are already daily practice in a variety of states.

---

*Calnan, M., Halik, J., and Sabbat, J., 'Citizen Participation and Patient Choice in Health Reform', in Saltman, R., Figneras, J., and Sakellairdes, C. (eds), *Critical Challenges for Health Care Reform in Europe.* Philadelphia: Open University Press, pp. 325–37, 1998.
†World Health Organisation regional Office for Europe, *The Rights of Patients in Italy*. WHO Regional Office for Europe, 1997.

Sweden is an example of a country where the delivery of health care is controlled by elected bodies. Sweden has a long tradition of local government with two tiers – first, the regional tier of 26 counties (or county councils), and below them nearly 300 municipalities. The self-governing county authorities, which are subject to election every third year, are responsible for the organisation and delivery of health services in line with national policy. Low electoral turnout is not an issue in Sweden. One in ten Swedish citizens plays an active part in the democratic process there, and nine out of ten citizens vote in regional and local elections (in which, unlike here, the standards and delivery of health care are issues). The Swedes show a great respect for their government, at all levels, due in part to the efforts that are made, both centrally and locally, to involve interested parties in debate and to create informed consensus.* In Norway, a chief county medical officer supervises the provision of health services by elected regional county and municipal authorities; in Spain, the very large regional 'autonomous communities' take responsibility for health services in compliance with basic principles set down by central government. In Finland, elected health boards, consisting of a mix of local lay people representing citizens' views as well as the chief physician from the municipal health centre, take responsibility for health services.†

It has to be noted that European practice is to give a greater role in public services to elected regional and local government. The trend in recent years has been towards greater devolution: even in states like France, which share the UK's centralist bias, local government has been reorganised with the introduction of regions. Smaller local authorities tend to be grassroots organisations, unlike the large local government units in the UK. Provision for local referenda, public services run by employee or user boards, citizens' decrees, one-off citizens' assemblies and other means of bringing about

---

*Jones, B., 'Sweden', in Wall, A. (ed.), *Health Care Systems in Liberal Democracies*. London: Routledge, pp. 104–26, 1966.
†Calnan, Halik and Sabbat, as above, p. 328.

citizens' involvement and participation are generally common, especially in Scandinavia. Proposals for elected boards in the NHS here would be common ground in most of the rest of Europe.

7

REFORMING THE NHS STRUCTURES

OUR CENTRAL PROPOSAL for reform of the NHS is that the service should be made more open and accountable through a constitution of its own. This proposal requires major changes in its current structures. The NHS as presently constituted is an opaque institution that is accountable upwards to the Secretary of State and Department of Health. The weaknesses we have detailed – from its complaints procedures to its practice over budgeting – are reflected in this pattern of accountability. The single most important change is to transform the NHS into an organisation that is at once responsible to the government and Secretary of State and at the same time semi-independent of both. Every degree of independence will inevitably make the NHS more transparent in its dealings with government and the public.

Our purpose is not to remove the ultimate authority over the NHS of an elected government, but to re-balance the relationship through an NHS constitution and a more arm's-length organisation. This proposal reflects the views of the public. The Commission's ICM opinion poll on the NHS asked the public to choose between giving the NHS 'a constitution of its own to define the government's duty to deliver free medical care at a time when people require it' and trusting 'elected politicians in government to safeguard the NHS's performance of this duty'. Nearly three-quarters of respondents – 69 per cent – wanted the NHS to have a constitution; just over a quarter (26 per cent) chose to put their trust in government ministers.

We have described how the service's position at the top, with an executive situated within the Department of Health accountable solely through the flawed mechanism of the ministerial responsibility of the Secretary of State to Parliament, makes both the policies and running of the NHS generally unaccountable. Ministers, officials within the department and NHS, and political advisers can evade proper Parliamentary scrutiny and public understanding by the combination of flexible ministerial powers and the secrecy within which central government makes and conducts policy. Further, at regional and local levels, as we have shown, the NHS is structured in ways that render its institutions opaque and out of reach. Mechanisms like the Patients Charter, the complaints procedures and annual public meetings are mere palliatives, and Community Health Councils, which could introduce a measure of accountability and openness, are too weak as presently constituted to do so.

It is for these reasons that the Commission has proposed that the NHS, the most prized of all public institutions, ought to be given a constitution as a fixed point of reference for ministers, officials, all NHS workers, institutions and administrators, parliamentarians and the public at large. However, an NHS constitution will be of little additional value within the current framework of the service. It is not in itself a single answer to the NHS's failings, nor a magic formula by which they can be remedied. It is rather a lodestar for a series of reforms in structure, conduct and ethos that will be necessary to transform the NHS into a more open, accountable and responsive service. Further, any such reforms must make sense on operational and managerial grounds; they must renew the sense of public service that inspires those who work within the service; they must strengthen the representation of ethnic minorities, women and people with disabilities in the system of governance; and they must similarly promote equality within the staff at all levels.

In a sense, our reforms are a kind of shock therapy. But we have taken care to ensure that the major changes we advocate are organic in spirit – especially those at the summit where government and the NHS now meet in secret – and command

73

broad public support. The structural changes we have considered to create a semi-independent NHS are all modelled on existing governing arrangements for the delivery of major public services.

Reform from the top

Reform must begin at the top with our alternative proposals for giving the NHS a constitution and operational independence under the ultimate authority of the Secretary of State and government, in line with the wishes of the public. There are four possible forms that a new NHS could assume – it could become:

A public corporation like the BBC and Bank of England;

An executive non-departmental public body (NDPB), or 'quango', like the Housing Corporation or Health and Safety Executive;

An executive (or 'Next Steps') agency like the Benefits Agency or Prison Service; or

A public corporation or executive NDPB with an elected board instead of an appointed board.

The least disturbing of these alternatives to the current order would be a shift to executive agency status. The existing NHS chief executive and the NHS Executive, made up entirely of government officials, would remain in charge, but outside the Department of Health, not inside it. The agency would be semi-autonomous but would legally remain part of the department. The Secretary of State and departmental officials would still make policy and allocate resources; while the chief executive, a civil servant even if appointed from outside, and his or her top officials would become responsible for all operational matters. In all the agencies set up so far, the Secretary of State agrees a 'framework agreement', or contract, with the agency chief executive. This document sets out the agency's aims and functions within the parameters of government policy. Under our proposal, the Secretary of State and NHS chief executive would agree a framework that observed the terms of the NHS constitution. The constitution would give the NHS a clear and public statement of principles and values, and a clearer mechanism for macro and micro accountability and public debate than any current executive agency possesses.

Existing agencies are hardly model accountable, transparent and responsive bodies. However, agency status would give the proposal for a constitution for the NHS an immediate administrative and political base, and offer modest gains in clarity, openness and accountability for Parliament and the public. Ministers and officials would be obliged publicly to set out the strategic objectives of the NHS, as specified under its constitution, and it would be possible to measure the NHS's progress in meeting them. The adequacy of the resources made available could be more clearly established and debated. The chief executive would emerge from the comparative obscurity of his or her present position inside the whale into the public domain and become more clearly answerable in Parliament. Relations between ministers, departmental officials and NHS bureaucrats would be opened up and the potential for further openness established, especially if the current Freedom of Information legislation made central government's policy-making processes more transparent and gave the Open Government Commissioner powers to review and overturn refusals to disclose information. Such changes could greatly reduce the lack of clarity that now leaves ministers and mandarins with a freedom of manoeuvre that is as serviceable to them as it is injurious to the public interest.

However, agency status in other service areas has brought about only modest gains in clarity and transparency, hardly any advance in accountability, and little substantive improvement in performance. The distinction between the government's responsibility for policy-making and the agency's responsibility for administration has remained blurred. We therefore advance the case for executive agency status as an incremental change for the better and the least objectionable from the point of view of government and the department. Even this modest change may however still be hard for either to swallow. Health ministers and officials have a major interest in retaining direct control. Were the NHS to become an executive agency, the department would 'lose' an important part of its being, and with it not only the size and prestige that the NHS confers, but also a largely unseen influence over the way the service is run. The loss of their discreet internal control of the NHS would deprive ministers and officials of the flexibility and discretion they prize, and remove their ability to fudge the crucial dividing lines between policy, resources and administration. They would have to set out the aims and objects of the NHS with clarity in public. It was precisely for these reasons that an internal government review of the case for transforming the NHS into an agency was firmly against the very idea.

The new NHS could become a major executive quango, or (more formally) a non-departmental public body (NDPB), like the Housing Corporation. As such it would possess a measure of independence from government and department, but would not be as independent as a public corporation, and would enjoy a lower status in the hierarchy of quasi-government. It would, however, benefit from its constitution, high public profile and intense interest in its affairs, all of which would bolster its independence. As a quango, it would have a board of its own, but under current arrangements board members would be appointed by the Secretary of State, albeit under the rules for public appointments set out by the Nolan Committee on Standards in Public Life. Under these rules the minister would have the final say on who is appointed and who is not. The constitution could of course set out additional rules governing the composition (for example, on the gender and ethnic mix, or balance of medical expertise) of the board.

Our preference is to make the NHS semi-independent as a public corporation, like the BBC or Bank of England. This would give the NHS a formal measure of arm's-length independence from government and department, with a higher status than either an executive agency or an executive quango, or NDPB, would have. The constitution and the high public profile that would accompany such high status would enhance the independence of a reformed NHS. This new NHS would have a board of its own, though, again, its members would be appointed by the government. A government is loosely bound by convention to keep a political balance in appointments to the BBC Board of Governors; and, as we argue above, the constitution could of course set out additional rules governing the composition of an NHS board, notably that it be representative of the entire community.

We also believe that the idea of a new NHS under an elected, or partly elected, board should remain an option, though probably in the longer term. We recognise the short-term need to recommend more incremental change, but we see no reason why a future government should not exploit the celebrated flexibility of governing arrangements in the UK by creating a new form of elected or part-elected public body, charged with safeguarding the service's constitution, running the NHS in conformity with the constitution and negotiating with the Secretary of State over the resources necessary to do so. Such a body could follow the model of a public corporation or NDPB. In considering this option, our greatest concern has been with the endemic conservatism of British public life and the pervasive distrust of election in governing circles. We are, however, confident that public interest in the NHS, as confirmed by our opinion poll, is strong enough to ensure that full, informed and meaningful elections to the new body would take place. Given the importance of the issues at stake and the value the public attaches to the NHS, we are confident that 'electoral fatigue' would not be a problem.

The regional dimension

Decisions taken at regional level are crucial both to the strategies of the NHS and to its effective performance. Such decisions, once within the remit of appointed regional health authorities (RHAs), are now taken unseen by regional offices of the NHS Executive. Our proposals should open up this tier of decision-making and administration to some measure of public scrutiny. We are in principle in favour of elected regional authorities throughout England to balance the devolved Parliament and assemblies in Scotland, Wales and Northern Ireland. Regional English assemblies would take strategic decisions on regional infrastructure, transport, land-use planning, employment, and so on, and major NHS decisions fall squarely within such a remit. Strategic decisions on the NHS and public health ought at least to be subject to scrutiny by elected regional authorities that could at the same time introduce an important element of democratic check and balance to the structure of the service. We prefer this long-term solution to any idea of reviving RHAs as elected bodies or turning them into regional quangos, but we regard it as very important that regional governance in the NHS should be made open to public scrutiny as soon as possible. As an interim measure, regional offices could be made subject to scrutiny by the indirectly elected regional chambers being set up in the English regions.

Health quangos

There is quite a variety of executive and advisory quangos, or non-departmental bodies (NDPBs) and special NHS bodies and authorities that deal with health issues within the Department of Health and the NHS. Their record on accountability and openness is patchy, even by standard official measures, though they are generally more accountable than the quangos of other departments. But they are not open to meaningful public access to their meetings, agendas, minutes and documents. And many of them perform vitally important public roles. The Committee for the Safety of Medicines and the Medicines Commission, for example, take decisions on drug safety and regulation that bear upon the health and safety of the public. These two bodies necessarily contain interested parties, operate largely behind closed doors and are not open to the public or peer-group review. It is a criminal offence to release information from either. But the public have almost full access to the meetings, data and decisions of their counterparts in the USA. At the very least, the sanction of criminal charges should be removed from disclosures of information about their proceedings; but ideally the public should be given full access to them and all other executive and advisory quangos, regulatory agencies and NHS bodies.

Reform at the bottom

Central to our view of reform at local level is the notion of replacing appointed bodies with elected authorities. By their very nature, appointed bodies are not publicly accountable to the populations they serve and are open to manipulation, both from above and from local elites. Were they purely administrative bodies, discharging instructions from on high, then there might be some case for leaving them unreformed. But they inevitably exercise a varying degree of discretion, making policy decisions and distributing resources that affect their client populations, and contributing to the evils of unsupervised postcode differences in health provision. Moreover, resource decisions, for example on hospital beds, can have a huge impact on local plans for community care and social services.

The case for introducing democracy at local level is not purely negative. Government in England has become centralised to a damaging degree, and the government's recently announced NHS reform strategy will concentrate central power still further. There is an urgent need to redress the imbalance between the centre and localities across the board, as well as in the NHS and community care. Citizens should be able to participate in and influence the decisions that affect their lives directly at local level. There is a need to connect up local decision-making on questions of health care, public health, social services, housing and other related matters. There is also an overwhelming case for reintroducing a productive political tension between decisions taken at national and local level. It is locally that policy, resource and funding decisions taken in Whitehall and its regional outposts really take effect; it is locally that most people are able to participate effectively in politics; and it is locally that people would be able to judge how well a reformed NHS was keeping to the promises of a new NHS constitution.

The public is generally in favour of replacing appointed authorities with elected or at least part-elected bodies. An ICM poll for Channel 4's 'Democracy Week' in 1994 showed a two-to-one (50 to 26 per cent) majority for elected over appointed health authorities, with another 18 per cent who wanted authority boards composed of elected members and appointed professionals. Our own ICM poll shows that the public are now less in favour of appointed health authorities (which attracted only 11 per cent), and even less enthusiastic about the idea of asking local authorities to take charge locally of the NHS (only 8 per cent support). Just over a third (34 per cent) chose a directly elected health authority, and two-fifths (41 per cent) a partly elected, partly appointed board.

Commentators often lament the ignorance of the public when it comes to their understanding of the major resource and rationing decisions that have to be taken within the NHS. But as we have demonstrated at length in this report, such decisions are generally taken out of sight, and are subject to political spin and counter-spin that is largely confined to contesting the respective funding regimes of the two major parties. A combination of clarity and openness at the top and democratic openness at the bottom would pave the way to public debate from experience on the proper allocation of resources to the NHS and the uses to which those resources are put. Elections to health authorities would foster greater knowledge of health issues.

However, there is a strong case for transferring the functions of health authorities to local government rather than making existing health authorities into elected, or part-elected, bodies in their own right. Local authorities are already functional elected bodies, and adding health to their portfolio would lead to 'joined-up government' at local level. Health and social services could be properly integrated and managed in concert. At present, the areas that health and social services serve are not necessarily coterminous, and where they are not, the interface between health and community care is weaker, more costly and more bureaucratic.

We tend to favour the alternative way of introducing local democratic governance to the NHS – that is, correcting the initial 'defect' in Bevan's 1948 plan and replacing 'selection with election', or part-election, directly to local health authorities. It can be argued that single-purpose elected authorities will be able to build on the existing knowledge and

80

experience of their appointed predecessors. They may also be more likely to adopt the open and responsive ethos that would be vital to their success than local authorities that are generally regarded by the public as remote and unresponsive bodies. Moreover, local authorities are beset by changing demands and responsibilities, and may not be capable of summoning the creative response necessary. Finally, the public treasure the NHS and may therefore be better motivated to vote for elections to NHS bodies rather than to the old local authorities with an extra responsibility.

We also note that a number of submissions made by professional associations within the NHS urged elected district and regional health authorities: the NHS Consultants' Association, for example, supports the principle of election to health authorities, arguing as we do that health should not have to compete with many of the other responsiblities of local government and it would be less likely to become polarised on party political lines. This is a view supported by organisations such as the Democratic Health Network and the NHS Consultants Association in their evidence to us.

If elected health authorities are seen as the way forward, we agree with the public that they should be partly elected, partly appointed, though we recommend that elected members should be in the majority, with appointed (or co-opted) members to provide specialist knowledge and to ensure balanced representation of minority groups. But there are other solutions. Howard Davis and Guy Daly, for example, have proposed that only the DHA chairs should be elected, as 'local health mayors', part of whose remit would be to make primary care group boards more widely representative.

Local voting and turnouts

Perhaps the biggest argument against either introducing further elections to health authorities at local level, or investing local government elections with more weight, is the fear of continuing low electoral turnouts. The turnout in existing local elections is low and seems to be falling; moreover, the local vote is generally a pale reflection of national political trends rather than a popular response to local policies and conditions. It remains to be seen whether the government's proposals to create a stronger bond between local authorities and their citizens, and proposals for elected mayors and other minor electoral reforms, will raise the rate of participation in local elections.

However, one main cause of this low turnout is first-past-the-post elections that tend to impose continuing party political oligarchies on local authorities and thus to reduce the point of voting either for the dominant party or for its under-represented rival parties. Another cause seems likely to be the general impotence of local authorities whose powers of initiative have been eroded by successive central governments, and which have been raised further and further away from local people through a series of reorganisations making them ever larger and so more remote from local communities. People may very well feel that there is hardly any point in voting for remote political representatives locally while real power resides at the centre.

Local elections in western Europe under proportional representation to smaller and more powerful local councils certainly produce higher turnouts than in the UK – we noted that in Sweden, where health is controlled by local govern-ment, turnout rates can rise as high as 90 per cent. It is likely that a major change of the kind we propose, taken in conjunction with a constitution for the NHS, will raise interest and the vote in local elections, either for enhanced local authorities or distinct health authorities. But either way, the rate of participation in elections would be increased, since people would be voting for local bodies important enough to make them worth voting for under a more representative electoral system.

NHS trusts and primary care trusts

Until recently, either elected health authorities or local authorities assuming the health portfolio could readily have absorbed the role of directing, funding and watching over the NHS trusts established under the previous government. This would have been a natural progression, and the trusts could well have remained largely appointed bodies, if with certain modifications to make them more skilled, more representative and formally more transparent and responsive to the public. But the government's new primary care groups (PCGs), which are now being introduced in England, complicate the issue.

These new bodies are designed to bring local health-care decisions closer to the public, but they present a major obstacle to ideas for grounding the NHS on a local, democratic base. Over time, they could even pose a threat to the principle of universal care under the NHS and to our putative NHS constitution. PCGs are to metamorphose into more autonomous primary care trusts (PCTs). PCGs are formally sub-committees of their health authorities, which nominate both a non-executive director and a 'lay person' to their boards. But the intention is that the semi-autonomous PCTs will become the major driving force in the NHS locally, whether publicly or privately run. Our view is that this initiative requires to be carefully monitored by government in the light of the growing concern about accountability within the NHS. If it is to continue to be the basis of a new deal locally, then at least democratic and regulatory safeguards should be introduced.

It is clear that the PCTs cannot easily be made responsible to elected health authorities (any more than they will be to appointed health authorities). Their shifting populations are not even coterminous with those of the health authorities to which they should supposedly be responsible. PCGs are currently required to enter into accountability agreements with health authorities, but the focus so far has largely been on financial accountability. It is perfectly possible to broaden this narrow scope to include accountability for adopting policies and practices endorsed by the local health authorities, for promoting equality and inclusive practice, for protecting the public interest in their progress, and so on. PCTs should be made formally answerable to their health authorities and should be required to become more democratic institutions in themselves. They are to have a majority of lay persons on their boards, but through processes of nomination, not election –

though we see no reason why they should not contain elected representatives of the patient body and obey rules of participation and consultation. Representative health authorities could assume overall responsibility for the composition of PCT trust boards to ensure that they are widely representative of the local populations and that no minority groups are explicitly or implicitly excluded. Their boundaries should be made contiguous those of the health authorities.

We further recommend that independent trust status should be removed from all present and future trusts, including PCTs; and that all local trusts and NHS bodies should be made accountable to elected health authorities (or perhaps the PCTs if they are made genuinely representative). All appointments to local NHS trusts and bodies should be advertised and made by nomination committees established by representative health authorities.

Appointments

Our proposals would greatly reduce the phalanxes of government appointees throughout the NHS. We have above recommended that appointments to local NHS and trusts should be under the control of representative health authorities. As for appointments at national level, we accept that ministers should continue to make significant appointments, subject to Nolan rules and further rules requiring balance in the composition of boards. But we agree with the Committee on Public Administration (CPA) that many less significant appointments could be made by an independent commission; and we believe that all appointments within the NHS should be liable to scrutiny by the Select Committee on Health and the CPA.

Ensuring equality in NHS structures

The first responsibility of a National Health Service is to serve the whole population equally. As argued above, equality means that everyone's needs are assessed and met on an equitable basis, regardless of race, gender, disability, sexuality, age, class or other difference; and that everyone has the chance of an equal say in determining how the service meets their group and own individual needs. Representative democracy through the ballot box is, as is coming to be recognised, too diffuse a process to guarantee equality in the NHS or other public services or in their governance. The government has agreed to impose a positive duty on public bodies to promote race equality. This duty will apply throughout the NHS, and it is very important that equality in all its aspects is built into its governance, service delivery and treatment of its staff.

Our proposals for reform of the structures of the NHS are based on a strengthening of the mechanisms of ministerial responsibility at the top and democratic renewal through the ballot box at local and, ultimately, regional level in England. But as we have seen throughout the elective polity, elections do not and cannot on their own ensure a proper mix of representatives in Parliament, the Scottish Parliament, Welsh Assembly, Northern Ireland Assembly (in spite of all the social engineering that went on there), or local authorities, in relation to ethnicity, gender, disability and so on. We therefore believe that our proposals for elected bodies should be qualified to leave space for fully scrutinised appointments to ensure a proper representative balance. There will also be a need for imaginative ways to consult minorities or those with special needs and to encourage them to participate in the provision of appropriate services, through CHCs, panels, subgroups and voluntary bodies. Effective training in equality and diversity will also be important throughout the service nationally to make all its institutions and staffs aware of the plurality of needs and demands that exists in our diverse nation; and to be sure that the NHS, as a major employer, delivers equality to women and minority populations. It is important that the need for equality and recognition of diversity is built into the very thinking of the national service, but this shift in conception will be especially important at the grassroots in the new PCGs and PCTs, for it is at this primary level that respect for equality and diversity must be most firmly established.

A draft National Health Constitution Act

The NHS

1 This Act shall be known as the Constitution for the National Health (NHS).

2 The NHS shall provide a comprehensive health service designed to secure improvement in the physical and mental health of the people of the United Kingdom and the prevention, diagnosis and treatment of illness, and for that purpose to provide or secure the effective provision of services in accordance with law.

The basic principles

3 The NHS shall be run in a way that so far as possible respects the basic principle of justice, which principle shall involve the following commitments:

   (i) that the NHS should be a universal service, available to all regardless of their means, ethnic origin, gender, age, sexuality or any other difference;

   (ii) that the services of the NHS should be free at the point of delivery;

   (iii) that the delivery of the services of the NHS should be informed by a commitment to equity and fairness, with everyone's needs to be assessed and met on an equitable basis.

4 The governance, management and administration of the NHS shall at all times be conducted in a way that respects the basic principle of good governance, which shall involve adherence to the following sub-principles:

   (i) the principle of representative government: that in so far as possible decisions affecting the public should be made by their representatives, that is, by those elected by them to exercise power on their behalf;

   (ii) the principle of informed public debate: open government at every level of decision-making, which in the context of the health service should certainly include policy formulation as well as the crystallisation of policy in firm written proposals;

   (iii) the principle of accountability: all decision-makers to be fully open and accountable for their actions.

(iv) the principle of equality: the governance, service delivery and employment practices of the NHS to promote equality and to monitor equality outcomes.

Application of the principles

5 The governance, management and administration of the NHS shall at all times be conducted in a way that is compatible with the basic principles set out at sections 3 and 4 above. Subject to sections 1–5 above, the Secretary of State or the relevant minister in any devolved administration within the United Kingdom shall from time to time:

(i) identify by ministerial order the precise ambit of the NHS within his or her jurisdiction;

(ii) set out in an appropriate form the policy framework within which the NHS is to operate within his or her jurisdiction;

(iii) allocate the resources that are to be made available to the NHS within his or her jurisdiction; and

(iv) establish such other bodies to assist in the discharge of his or her duties as he or she judges necessary or appropriate.

6 Within the framework set out at sections 1–5 above, the execution of national policy within the NHS shall be the primary responsibility of a public corporation (or an elected board or a new executive non-departmental public body).

7 The implementation of policy within the NHS at the local level shall be the responsibility of elected regional and health authorities, whose composition, function and relationship with the central administration of the NHS are detailed in the accompanying text with provision for appointments to ensure appropriate balance. In furtherance of the principles set out at sections 3 and 4 above, Community Health Councils shall have statutory watchdog rights with a national association funded centrally by government.

8 In furtherance of the principles set out at sections 3 and 4

above, there shall be a patients' charter to which all those involved in the NHS shall have regard.

9   All complaints within the NHS concerning its operation shall be dealt with in accordance with the basic principles of good governance and natural justice, and in the manner described in the accompanying text.

10   The Health Ombudsman shall have a general duty to investigate any failure to meet the terms of the NHS constitution by medical staff.

11   This Constitution shall not be altered except by Act of Parliament.

12   All legislation (including delegated legislation) passed or to be passed shall be interpreted so far as possible so as to be compatible with this Constitution, and in particular with the principles of justice and good governance set out at sections 2 and 3. The final arbiter of this compatibility will be the House of Commons Select Committee on Health.

13   The House of Commons Select Committee on Health (and the analogous bodies in areas of the UK with devolved administrations) shall report annually to the House of Commons on the state of the NHS.

8

THE LAW, REDRESS AND THE NHS

THE FIRST QUESTION that arises about the role of law in relation to a reformed NHS is how far the proposed constitution should be directly enforceable in the courts. There are many reasons for enlisting judicial protection. The courts are traditionally the place where written constitutions are protected and developed. The right of any citizen or resident to hold his or her health service accountable in law for the principles and priorities to which it has committed itself is an attractive proposition. Enforcing the NHS's basic constitution in the courts seems to offer a means of guaranteeing NHS services that would be above the political fray and detached from any passing political, economic or ideological crisis.

Despite these apparent strengths, we do not believe that the protection of the new NHS constitution should be the primary responsibility of the courts. Of course the judges will be bound to exert some oversight of the system we are proposing, so that the terms of the Act of Parliament setting out the constitution are not wholly flouted or abused. But the primary protection of the new constitution of the NHS should remain firmly within the political domain. Judges are not well equipped in terms of their training or resources to take on the job of policing the new NHS constitution; and judicial review is a process with important limitations.* The certainty offered

*See Sunkin et al., *Judicial Review in Perspective*. Public Law Project report, 1993.

by sole reliance on the law would be more apparent than real: pressures on the system would find their way into judicial rulings, in the form of a dilution of standards or some other restructuring of what appeared in the framework document. Nor do judges possess any kind of democratic legitimacy, a point that we cannot ignore when seeking to construct a more democratic health service. Not only should the service we are designing be more democratic, but the primary systems that we put in place to protect the new NHS from abuse should also be firmly rooted in a democratic base.

What we propose is that the NHS constitution should in the first instance be protected by the continuing oversight for the UK as a whole of the Select Committee on Health, strengthened by additional resources and the power of the constitution, and by similar committees in the Scottish Parliament and devolved assemblies in Wales and Northern Ireland. The function of such committees would be: to keep the operation of the NHS in their area of responsibility under continuous review; to hold inquiries of both a general and a particular nature at their discretion into its policies, practice and resourcing; to consider and report on whether any changes are required to the NHS constitution; to consider and if necessary commission legal advice as to whether the conduct of any element of the NHS within their realm of responsibility was in conflict with the constitution; and to report. In time, we look forward to health committees on new English regional assemblies.

The hearings and reports of such committees would provide a new political focus for the NHS. The variety of such committees under the UK's new devolved system of government would reduce the risk of the committees falling under the deadening, whip-driven influence of the government of the day. There would remain a role for the law as a long-stop guardian of constitutional propriety, and as a guarantee of procedural rights such as access to information and to proper consultation on decision-making, but the primary focus for the protection of the NHS constitution would be rightly centred on the political process, i.e., on the representatives of the people for whose benefit that constitution has been designed.

The Select Committee on Health should at the same time be strengthened in two ways: first, the committee should be fully resourced for its role as a parliamentary watchdog; and second, the Health Ombudsman should report to this committee, as well as to the Committee on Public Administration, at least on cases that raise systemic issues. In turn, artificial restrictions on the inquiries that the Health Ombudsman may take should be removed: in particular he should be empowered both to inquire into the policy aspects of his caseload, and to initiate inquiries as he sees fit, and he should be given the resources necessary to follow up earlier recommendations.

We also recommend that the National Audit Office and Audit Commission should possess similar powers to take their inquiries beyond practice and the facts of a case to the policies that lie behind them.

Complaints and redress

It is clear that the NHS complaints procedures require urgent reform. We are dismayed by their lack of independence and rigour. Their aim is to promote conciliation rather than thorough inquiry, individual justice and redress. The purpose of the procedures must be redefined to make justice and redress for complainants their first priority. We recommend that all complaints from patients and their families should be handled by genuinely independent review panels. There is even a case for the panels to be constituted like juries. All staff who deal with complainants should be clearly independent of the institutions complained of, and trained to ensure that they behave in an appropriately fair and impartial way. There should also be a fair, impartial and effective complaints procedure for all patients who receive private health care, whether they are paying themselves or have been referred from the public health service.

Complainants should be empowered to bring complaints formally; to take their complaints further if they are dissatisfied with the initial adjudication; and to receive compensation for wrongdoing. The recommendation of panels should be binding unless they are appealed against. These seem rudimentary first principles of natural justice, but they are not yet the basis of NHS complaints procedures.

The capacity of the Health Ombudsman to provide redress is particularly weak. He operates within an institutional straitjacket, designed to protect the policies of government and the dignity of MPs. He is unable to initiate investigations and has no powers to insist on seeing government information. The rule that he can act only when the NHS complaints procedures are exhausted severely limits access to his services. We recommend above that the artificial limits on his freedom of action should be removed to ensure that his investigations take policy and resources issues into account and reveal systemic weaknesses. Such changes should also assist him in providing individual justice and compensation. Further, complainants should have clearly defined rights of appeal to the Ombudsman from disputed decisions by independent panels. The Ombudsman should be able to call evidence and witnesses; to make binding rulings; and to award financial compensation.

Whatever complaints procedures are in place, many patients or families with complaints will require informed advice and, if necessary, advocacy. The network of Community Health Councils and equivalent bodies in Scotland (see chapter 5) have played an advisory and advocacy role for a quarter of a century. They were first established in 1974 to provide a lay voice in the NHS and make up for its evident 'democratic deficit'. But they were also asked to act as watchdogs for patients' interests. We do not regard CHCs as a substitute for democracy in the health service, but we have come to the conclusion that they can play an invaluable role as advocates for dissatisfied consumers and as independent and informed watchdogs at local level. They also provide a way to involve concerned members of the public as volunteers in the development of the service on a long-term, comprehensive and participatory basis.

As we saw in chapter 5, CHCs have a chequered past and have been forced to make their considerable contribution to the NHS from uncertain foundations. We considered whether the functions of this largely voluntary network ought to be taken over by other statutory, elected or quasi-public agencies. But with the model of the great voluntary – and analogous – national network of Citizens' Advice Bureaux in mind, we decided that CHCs should be strengthened, whether or not our other recommendations are followed. Indeed, if they are not, then the case for stronger CHCs becomes compelling.

CHCs, like CABs, have gained the trust of the public. We believe that this trust provides a basic measure of legitimacy to the whole organisation, though we advise the CHCs never to take that trust for granted and to make themselves as open and pluralist an operation as they can.

The over-arching national organisation, the Association of Community Health Councils of England and Wales (ACHCEW), is a statutory national co-ordinating and training body for CHCs, but its position is vulnerable. As we have seen, it depends for its funding on the voluntary local CHCs, which can withdraw from membership. The central association cannot require them to observe uniform standards or train their volunteers, but has to rely on persuasion and disseminating information on best practice. The relationship between the centre and local CHCs needs to be re-balanced. The starting point is to establish a stronger, centrally funded national association with an arm's-length relationship with the Secretary of State. But the association must remain independent both of government and the NHS.

A newly empowered and accountable ACHCEW could play an invaluable role in providing information and training to CHCs; maintaining standards of service; establishing a collectively agreed role for CHCs; and collating comparative data from CHCs to report back on a national level about standards of care in the NHS, the evenness of services, etc., on the ground. In short, CHCs should perform the role set out by Frank Dobson, as Secretary of State, in 1998, to act as the representative of the public and individual patients at national and local level. The value of this kind of audit, based directly on people's experience around the country, has been demonstrated by NACAB, the National Association of CABs, as well as by ACHCEW itself.

The key to giving ACHCEW a national co-ordinating role is resources. There is something to be said for funding via local CHCs, but the instability and low level of resources that such funding alone generates is profoundly harmful. ACHCEW should be funded centrally out of general taxation for certain major aspects of this role, such as providing training and maintaining standards. At local level, CHCs' once statutory right to be consulted on substantial variations in health policies and practice needs to be re- established on a statutory footing. The opaque and unsatisfactory process by which CHC objections to policy changes go to the Secretary of State for adjudication needs to be opened to public gaze and debate.

Further, the gradual erosion of the other limited statutory rights of CHCs needs to be remedied. They should be given oversight of all premises on which public health care is provided, even if they are privately run. They should be asked to monitor the recuperative and rehabilitative work that has moved from acute hospitals to patients' homes. Their traditional observer status, with speaking rights, at meetings of health authorities should also be established as of right vis-à-vis the dynamic new 'purchasers' of care locally, the primary care groups, soon to be trusts. We recommend that the NHS Executive, and any successor body, should review all legislation and changes in structure and practice over the past twenty-five years to protect the watchdog role of CHCs; and that they should have a formal relationship with the Commission for Health Improvement, with powers to initiate a CHI inquiry into local health policy under well-defined criteria.

We take the view that health authorities ought to continue to expand their efforts to consult and involve the public through citizens' juries and other means (see chapter 3). But they ought to be encouraged to regard CHCs as partners, recognising that CHCs perform a valuable role on behalf of the public because they are independent of the NHS while being part of it. We set detailed recommendations on the future of CHCs in Annex 4.

Professional accountability

The remit of all the professional associations that regulate and train health professionals should be expanded to ensure that high standards of care are maintained by their members and provide an effective system of redress for patients. Lay representatives should be introduced by law on to their governing bodies.

Their self-regulatory frameworks have been established ad hoc over time. There is little consistency among them, and none is strong enough to meet the current pressures and demands for accountability, scrutiny and redress. The two leading agencies – the GMC and the UKCC – are seeking to upgrade their efforts to disseminate best practice, to increase lay representation and to become proactive in their monitoring of professional standards. The Royal Colleges and other regulatory agencies are moving in the same direction. We recommend that the growing trend towards proactive regulation and redress should be formalised into proper mechanisms of regulation, redress and accountability through the NHS constitution that we propose. Our instinct is not to call for root-and-branch reform, but to build on the current structures.

We have observed that professional regulatory frameworks in health care are designed to deal with the matter of the fitness to practise of individual practitioners of the professions, and do not address systemic issues that affect standards of professional care. Yet it is important to build a wider accountability to consumers of health care and the general public into these frameworks. We recommend the following general principles to the government and professional self-regulatory agencies in health care:

A statutory basis for professional regulation.
Formal recognition by each professional regulatory body of its accountability to the public and patients.
Regular (at least every five years) re-registration, revalidation or review of individual practitioners with consumer representation in the process.

Substantial consumer representation on each regulatory body. The adoption of a consumer-involvement strategy by each association, with appropriate staffing to make it work. An emphasis in initial and post-qualification training on the primary responsibility of each practitioner to secure and promote the best interests of consumers of health care.

Voluntary organisations

Voluntary organisations of various kinds have for two centuries or so played a prominent role nationally and locally in public life in the United Kingdom, and particularly in providing social services. Their social-service role actually expanded after the development of the welfare state, even though the NHS was established as a national state service.

Voluntary organisations providing health care and associated services are accountable to the health authorities with which they have contracts for these services. Most, however, also see themselves as being primarily accountable to the users of these services. Voluntary organisations campaigning for improved health services often seek to represent users. If they are user-organisations, they may be said to be self-governing. In this sense, they are accountable to a particular interest group rather than to the public in general. The Commission welcomes the healthy voluntary movement in and around the NHS, and appreciates the contribution the various organisations jointly and severally make to public welfare and public debate. They can continue to play a service and ginger-group role in relation to a more democratic and open NHS, and that role may well prove more valuable in such circumstances. But it has to be balanced by a wider and more representative public input into the public debate on health.

9

THE CONSTITUTION AND HEALTH CHOICES

IN CHAPTER 1 WE discussed how terms like rationing, efficiency and value for money are laden with implicit value judgements, even intruding into apparently technical discussions about the pros and cons of hypothecated taxes or private health insurance. Obviously the Commission wants to get good value from every pound that is spent in the health service, but we have stressed that assessing what is value is more than a task for accountants and economists. It involves a complex assessment of our collective priorities, and this in turn requires giving people a voice in the decisions that are made on their behalf. This lies at the heart of our case for a constitution for the NHS.

Of course decisions on the level of funding for the NHS would remain squarely with the government of the day, which would be held accountable via the ballot box if it misjudged the mood of the electorate on the proper balance between taxation levels and expenditure on health and other public goods. On this issue, the constitution we propose would merely impose standards of clarity on the reporting of funding decisions to prevent double-counting and other pieces of financial legerdemain that we described in earlier chapters. It would also allow the public to judge whether proposals like the Private Finance Initiative or the current Primary Care Groups and Trusts offend the constitutional principles that NHS managers and ministers alike must respect.

The attempt to unmask our value judgements and bring

clarity into the relationship between cost and projected benefit is at the heart of the economists' notion of the 'social welfare' function. But in order to have any idea of what society's collective social welfare function might be, we need the correct information and then the means to express our preferences and trade-offs.

We have argued in chapter 1 that we are sceptical about the inevitability of rationing on a scale that would require overturning the principles upon which we believe the NHS should rest. However, it is true that because each pound can only be spent once, decisions need to be made about what takes priority over what. The public need to understand the way the costs are determined and allocated so that the priorities made by decision-makers on their behalf are out in the open. That cancer and heart treatment should be a priority will be commonly understood. But what priority, for example, should preventive medicine and better public health take in overall budget decision-making?

The question of transparency is no less urgent. Over the last twenty years long-term care, rehabilitation and convalescent care provision – inevitably more concentrated on the elderly – have been made largely a private responsibility with almost no public debate. This policy would have offended the basic principles of our proposed constitution and would therefore have been impossible, at least without much better safeguards and protection than exist at present. Indeed the whole question of the NHS's treatment of the elderly needs to be brought out into the open: much of the individual evidence to the Commission was from people scandalised by the treatment of elderly relatives in hospitals or long-term care. Is this the choice – or social welfare function in economic terminology – that the community wishes to make? We note that a year after the Royal Commission on Long Term Care reported the government has still to act. The fundamental purpose of the NHS, after all, is to guarantee every citizen of whatever age, gender or race the best treatment – inevitably involving a measure of redistribution from the healthy to the unhealthy. But such redistribution is at the heart of the explicit health social contract.

In an ideal world, a social welfare function would govern how such agonising decisions are made by specifying the trade-offs between competing demands for resources. Determining such trade-offs is a political hot potato for an elected government, and the temptation for a party politician is therefore always to fudge the issues – which means, in practice, that the trade-offs are decided by unaccountable bureaucrats further down the line of command. Part of our reason in proposing an NHS constitution, and other measures that would have the effect of distancing the governance of the NHS from the party political process, is the need to ensure that decisions over the necessary trade-offs are explicit and up-front.

Clarity on funding levels and establishing our priorities for spending and preferred benefits are only the first steps in ensuring value for money in the NHS. The remaining steps are likely to be much more difficult, requiring an ongoing evolution in the economic organisation of the NHS that will take many years, not least addressing sources of private power, like the drug companies whose own preferences and objectives distort those of the wider society. We perceive a broad consensus both on the necessity for such a continuing programme of reform and on its general outline. However, hotly disputed differences over matters of detail can easily derail a project whose underlying principles are not explicitly stated, and so we think it useful to comment on what we think the principles should be.

The key to better decision-making is to delegate as much as possible within generally agreed rules and objectives. It is uncontroversial that an economically efficient structure in a complex environment always involves decentralising the power to make decisions to where the necessary knowledge and expertise resides. We do not want accountants telling doctors how to extract an appendix, or doctors instructing accountants on double-entry book-keeping. But nor can each expert or specialist be left to do their own thing as they see fit. Their efforts need to be co-ordinated and their information pooled if the objectives built into the social welfare function are to be achieved. There is a well-established economic discipline of 'mechanism design' in which this aim is engineered by setting up a system of rules that constrain the actions of a decision-maker that a boss can understand and monitor effectively. In the case of actions that cannot be effectively monitored, or that lie outside the boss's area of expertise, the solution is to provide an appropriate system of incentives that lead decision-makers to act in accordance with our collective preferences rather than following their own personal inclinations.

Improving the design of the system of rules and incentives that govern the NHS is a daunting scientific task that deserves substantially more resources than it currently receives. No aeronautic engineer would strap a pair of wings to her back and leap off a high building to see if they work. She would devise theoretical models to guide her design, and test them out in wind-tunnels before even thinking about leaping off the smallest of buildings. We believe that the NHS should be doing the same kind of thing before taking flight with a new reform. For example, the NHS did test the 'internal market', but it did no more than run two computerised game simulations in an imaginary Healthshire. Even this experiment proved how risky the internal market would be, the players reporting that 'catastrophe was narrowly avoided'. But such was the ideological push to deliver the market that the results were brushed aside.

Researching and testing proposed reforms is certainly expensive and time-consuming, but our health is too important for corners to be cut. We understand that one has to make hard choices when responding to crises, but surely the time has come for less crisis management and more long-term strategic planning in the NHS. We believe our constitution would provide a framework within which such an approach could become a reality.

One reason for exceeding our remit by reiterating the obvious but all too often disregarded principles of efficient mechanism design is that they apply not only to health professionals within the NHS, but also to ourselves, as members of the public interacting with the health service and its management. We need to recognise that we must be involved ourselves in monitoring those aspects of the NHS that we are qualified to judge, because no internal system of rules and incentives can ever be fully effective without outside scrutiny. Nor should we forget that those who act on our behalf in monitoring the system need to be incentified themselves. The respect and interest of the rest of us will go a long way in this direction.

CONCLUSION

AT THE HEART of our report lies one big idea: that the moment has arrived for the NHS to be given a constitution that sets out the principles and practices by which we, the British, expect this great institution to be run. We are not asking for the NHS to be independent of the political process, or to avoid highly charged political decisions about how it should be funded or to become embroiled in judge-made law. The Secretary of State for Health will remain a pivotal figure. But we are arguing that in an environment where public institutions are being afforded more independence, where self-regulation is giving way to more statutory and professional regulation, and where the public is growing more critical and less compliant, a grudging piecemeal approach to absorbing these trends will fail. Giving the NHS greater constitutional independence meets all these requirements in one encompassing act.

We emphasise that it builds on existing trends and thinking in British society. It may at first sight seem a radical or even Utopian proposal; but reflect for a moment. The trends that we have identified in this report exist and are likely to intensify in the years ahead. The Ombudsman's unsatisfactory powers; the weakness of Community Health Councils; the lack of natural justice in NHS complaints procedures; the clamour for more information about how budgets are determined and priorities set; the growing protest at the inadequacy and sometimes brutalities of British health provision – none of these have been invented by the Commission.

They are realities about the contemporary health service, and in our view they sap its legitimacy and vitality.

A constitution allows these new demands to be met head-on. And if we are criticised for our commitment to principles like free, equal and universal provision, then we take the view that some of the zeal and passion that drove the founding fathers of the health service needs to be recaptured today. If the NHS is not a principled institution, then it is nothing. If we want to improve the morale and commitment to patient service of every man and woman in the NHS, there seems no better route than insisting that their vocation is special and that we are prepared to enshrine that belief in an NHS constitution.

We were not asked to make recommendations about funding, rather about the processes by which funding is decided. It is clear to us that what is needed is renewed trust in the NHS's capacity to use whatever resources it has wisely, and that the criteria by which it sets priorities have to be established as those in which we all believe. That is the purpose of a constitution. It obliges the NHS to behave according to clearly articulated principles on which it is held to account at every level, and so helps to take every anguished accident, mishap and no-win policy choice away from the national political arena, where it does not belong. Accountability is thus woven into its warp and woof, from complaints procedures to its dealings with multinational drug companies.

And once the idea of a constitution is accepted, the notion of voting for some of the members of regional and health boards – even that of the NHS itself – becomes less exotic. Voting, for all our British reserve, remains the chief means of expressing public opinion in Western democracies and of exercising accountability. We note the support for this idea in our opinion poll.

Our constitution does not pretend to be a blueprint. It is one variant among a number of possibilities. But we do believe that the time has come for the NHS to be granted its constitutional independence, and that the debate about the hows and means should begin. Indeed, at a time when the

103

conception of Britishness is held to be under assault, the process of building a British constitution for the NHS will be an important reminder of what we British hold in common. We offer this report to our fellow citizens as a proposal to be democratically discussed – not a tablet of stone handed down by so-called experts. We believe it holds the answer to resolving the current crisis in the NHS. We hope you agree.

Annex 1: Members of the Commission

Will Hutton (Chair) Will Hutton was appointed chief executive of the Industrial Society in February 2000. He was previously editor of the *Observer* from March 1996 to July 1998, and then its Editor-in-Chief. His best-selling book *The State We're In*, an economic and political analysis of the state of Britain, was first published in 1995. His most recent book, *On the Edge*, co-edited with Professor Anthony Giddens, was published in March this year. Other books include *The State to Come*, *The Stakeholding Society* and *The Revolution That Never Was*. A former stockbroker, Will Hutton worked as an economics correspondent, producer and director at the BBC from 1978 to 1988, including five years as economics editor of BBC2's Newsnight. He joined the *Guardian* in 1990 as Economics Editor, and was appointed Assistant Editor in 1995. He was named as 'Political Journalist of the Year' by Granada TV's 'What the Papers Say' for his coverage of the 1992 ERM crisis. Amongst other duties Will Hutton is a governor of the London School of Economics and chair of the Employment Policy Institute, a think-tank on employment matters.

Professor Ken Binmore (from July 1999) Ken Binmore is Director of the ESRC Centre for Economic Learning and Social Evolution, and Leverhulme Research Professor at University College, London. His experience as an economist and researcher into the design of economic systems includes leading the team responsible for the recent multi-billion pound UK telecom auction. His books include the recent *Playing Fair: Game Theory and the Social Contract*. His research work extends beyond economics to mathematics, psychology and political philosophy.

Professor Conor Gearty Conor Gearty is Professor of Human Rights Law at King's College, London, and a member of Matrix Chambers. He is the author of numerous books and articles on human rights and civil liberties, including (with K. D. Ewing) *Freedom Under Thatcher and Civil Liberties in Modern Britain* (1990). His most recent book, *The Struggle for Civil Liberties: Political Freedom and the Rule of Law in Britain, 1914–45*, co-authored with K. D. Ewing, was published in February 2000 by Oxford University Press.

Susie Parsons Susie Parsons is Chief Executive of the Commission for Racial Equality. Her work experience spans the health service, local government and the voluntary sector. Having begun her working life as a teacher of French in an inner-city school in London, she subsequently held the posts of Director of Community Education for Shelter, Housing Projects Officer at North Kensington Law Centre, Secretary to Paddington and North Kensington Community Health Council, General Manager of the London Energy and Employment Network, and Head of Press, Publicity and Information for the London Borough of Hackney. She was appointed to the post of Executive Director of London Lighthouse in September 1994 and became its Chief Executive in January 1997. She has written extensively on subjects ranging from community education to women in management and health and social care.

Professor Allyson Pollock Allyson Pollock is head of the Health Services and Health Policy Research Unit at the School of Public Policy, University College, London, and Director of Research and Development at University College London Hospitals Trust. She trained in medicine in Scotland and worked in hospitals in Edinburgh and Leeds before moving to London in 1987. She spent a year in the United States in 1995–6 as a Harkness Fellow. She has researched and published widely on a number of areas including health policy, rationing, cancer epidemiology, long-term care and the private finance initiative.

Joyce Struthers Joyce Struthers was elected Chair of the Association of Community Health Councils for England and Wales (ACHCEW) in July 1998. She is ACHCEW's representative on the Management Board of the BMA's Doctor/Patient Partnership and on the Middlesex University Ethical Committee for the Practice of Traditional Chinese Medicine. She served as a generalist member of North Bedfordshire Health Authority from 1985 to 1989, and soon afterwards became a member of the North Bedfordshire CHC, which she chaired from 1992 to 1996. She was a Marriage Guidance (now Relate) counsellor, 1971–83; a voluntary worker in the Bedfordshire Divorce Conciliation Service, 1982–94; Vice President of Bedfordshire Care Support Network for People with Learning Disabilities, 1989–97; and has worked as an approved Lay Assessor with the Quality Control and Inspection Unit of Bedfordshire County Council's Social and Community Care Department. She is the CHC observer on the Bedfordshire Strategic Health Board and the Bedfordshire County Council Quality Control Advisory Committee.

Professor Stuart Weir Stuart Weir is Senior Research Fellow at the Human Rights Centre, University of Essex, and Director of the Democratic Audit at the university; an international Consultant and Training Adviser on Democracy and Human Rights with the Department for International Development, International IDEA (Institute for Democracy and Electoral Assistance), Stockholm; the European Union; and British Council. He is an active journalist in television and print. He is currently engaged on projects to measure democracy and governance for DFID and International IDEA. He is co-author of two major studies on human rights and democracy in the United Kingdom, *The Three Pillars of Liberty* (with Francesca Klug and Keir Starmer) and *Political Power and Democratic Control in Britain* (with David Beetham), and has collaborated in influential series of studies of quangos and elections in Britain. He was previously a journalist, editor of the *New Statesman*, and founder of Charter 88, the campaign for constitutional reform in the United Kingdom.

Stephen Thornton, Chief Executive of the NHS Confederation, was a member of the Commission until June 1999, when he withdrew because of pressure of work and the expectation that the Commission's work would continue into 2000. He was right.

Secretariat

Angeline Burke   Association of Community Health Councils for England and Wales.
Frances Presley   Association of Community Health Councils for England and Wales.

ANNEX 2: NHS STRUCTURES AND GOVERNANCE

Department of Health/NHS Executive (NHSE)
The Department of Health is headed by the Secretary of State, supported by Ministers and the NHS Policy Board. This Board is responsible for providing independent policy advice and supporting the Secretary of State in holding the NHS Executive to account for its management of the NHS. Members of the Board come from within and outside the NHS. The NHS Executive is the operational wing of the Department of Health. It is headed by the Chief Executive of the NHS, who is the principal policy adviser to the Secretary of State on all matters relating to the NHS. The Executive Board is made up of the directors of the Regional Offices and all NHS Executive directors.

Eight Regional Offices, staffed by civil servants, act as regional and local agents of the NHS Executive. The Regional Offices are responsible for monitoring the performance of purchasers and providers, and managing the implementation of national NHS policies and priorities, and overseeing the commissioning of regional specialities. In addition the Regional Offices are responsible for the establishing arrangements for Community Health Councils.

Regional Health Authorities – RHAs (until 1 April 1996)
Each RHA had a Chair and five non-executive members appointed by the Secretary of State, together with up to five executive members. Two of the executive members, the general manager and the chief finance officer were ex-officio

members. The remainder were appointed by the Chair and non-executives together with the general manager. The RHA was accountable to the Secretary of State.

Accountability of the Department of Health

The Secretary of State is accountable to Parliament for the policies and actions of the Department of Health and the provision of a National Health Service.

The House of Commons Health Committee is able to examine the expenditure, administration and policy of the Department of Health and associated public bodies. It consists of a number of Members of Parliament with membership reflecting the overall number of MPs in each political party.

The Public Accounts Committee of the House of Commons, supported by the Comptroller and Auditor General and the National Audit Office, calls the NHS to account for the way the NHS budget is spent.

The Audit Commission is an independent statutory body that audits NHS and local government spending and examines value for money in the use of resources.

The Health Service Ombudsman has responsibility and powers to investigate charges of maladministration in the NHS and will take up complaints from members of the public when these fall into the remit of the Ombudsman's office. The Ombudsman publishes the results of these inquiries and is required to report to the House of Commons Public Administration Committee.

Health Authorities

Health authorities' key tasks are:
• Assessing the health needs of their local population.
• Drawing up strategies for meeting those needs.
• Determining local targets and standards to drive up quality and efficiency in the light of national priorities and guidance.
• Supporting Primary Care Groups/Local Health Groups in their area, allocating their resources and holding them to

account. The health authority has a lay Chair appointed by the Secretary of State and a Board of appointed executive and non-executive members. The non-executive lay members have a majority on the Board. Each health authority is accountable to a Regional Office or the Welsh Office for carrying out its statutory functions.

Special Health Authorities

Special Health Authorities (SHAs) administer some NHS services in England, for example, the National Blood Authority. They are accountable directly to the Secretary of State.

Trusts

NHS trusts run hospitals and NHS services and their appointed Boards are made up of executive and non-executive directors. The Regional Offices monitor their performance. Trusts are required to hold their Board meetings in public.

Primary Care Groups/ Primary Care Trusts

As sub-committees of health authorities, PCG Boards are accountable through their Chair to the Chief Executive of the health authority. PCGs are required to take a number of measures, for example, to produce annual accountability agreements in order to promote a measure of openness and accountability. PCGs will eventually evolve into Primary Care Trusts, and a few have already done so. PCTs will have the same mechanism of accountability as other trusts.

Commission for Health Improvement

A Commission for Health Improvement was established in November 1999 to oversee clinical governance. It is a non-departmental public body (NDPB), or quango, and has an appointed board. It will offer an independent guarantee that local systems to monitor, measure and improve clinical quality are in place, and will be able to intervene on the direction of the Secretary of State or by invitation from PCGs, health authorities and trusts.

The Department of Health also sponsors seven executive NDPBs, or quangos, 38 advisory NDPBs, some of which perform a regulatory function, and three tribunals. These are all appointed bodies. There are also 16 NHS bodies, other than Health Authorities and Trusts and NICE, such as the National Blood Authority, the Ashworth and Rampton Hospital Authorities, and the NHS Supplies Authority.

Northern Ireland

In Northern Ireland the Department of Health, Social Services and Public Safety (HPSS) is required to secure the provision of an integrated service designed to promote the health and social care of the population. The HPSS Management Group is headed by a Deputy Secretary with responsibility for five directorates. These are Secondary Care, Primary Care and Commissioning Development, Child and Community Care, Planning and Performance Management and Human Resources Directorate. Four Health and Social Services Boards act as agents for the HPSS. They have a non-executive Chair, six non-executive and six executive directors. The non-executive directors are appointed by the Minister, but the appointment of the Chair has to be with the approval of the Secretary of State.

Health and Social Services Trusts (HSS Trusts) provide health and social services. Each is managed by a Board that has up to five non-executive directors and a non-executive Chair who is appointed by the HPSS with the approval of the Secretary of State. In addition there are five executive members who are employees of the Trusts.

Health and Social Services Councils perform similar functions to Community Health Councils in England and Wales.

Scotland

The Scottish Parliament is responsible for the NHS in Scotland. However, important reserve powers are held in Westminster. These include pay, education, training and regulation of health-care professionals. The Cabinet of the Scottish Parliament, which includes the Minister for Health and Community Care, has a full programme of primary and secondary health-care legislation. Health boards and NHS Trusts are accountable to the Scottish NHS Management Executive and to the Minister.

The Parliament has also established a Health and Community Care committee which is holding the health service to account, in terms of legislation, policy and practice. They do not have powers of enforcement, but their recommendations are hard to ignore. There is a regular question time in which Members of the Scottish Parliament can ask searching questions about local health-care issues. There is, moreover, a Public Petitions Committee, through which the public can raise issues. Recently a public protest meant that a health board was called to account through this committee. The Scottish Association of Health Councils believes that the health service in Scotland is far more accountable to the public since devolution.

Local Health Councils perform similar functions to Community Health Councils in England and Wales. However, they have a different membership appointment system and are broadly coterminous with health boards.

Wales

In Wales there is no intermediate management tier. The five health authorities work directly with the Health Department of the National Assembly of Wales in policy and management areas. Accountability is via performance agreements and an annual review.

The National Assembly of Wales is responsible for decision-making but does not have primary legislation powers. It does have powers to make secondary legislation.

ANNEX 3: THE COUNCIL OF EUROPE RECOMMENDATION ON PARTICIPATION IN HEALTH CARE

Decision-making processes

Recommendation No. R (2000) 5 of the Committee of Ministers of the Council of Europe to its Member States on the Development of Structures for Citizen and Patient Participation in the Decision-Making Process affecting Health Care was adopted on 24 February 2000 at the 699th meeting of the Ministers' Deputies.

The full text of the Recommendation is as follows:

The Committee of Ministers, under the terms of Article 15.b of the Statute of the Council of Europe,

Considering that the aim of the Council of Europe is to achieve greater unity between its members and that this aim may be pursued, inter alia, by the adoption of common action in the public health field;

Bearing in mind Article 11 of the European Social Charter on the right to the protection of health;

Recalling Article 3 of the Convention on Human Rights and Biomedicine requiring the Contracting Parties to provide 'equitable access to health care of appropriate quality', and Article 10 on the right of everyone to know any information about his or her health;

Having regard to the Convention for the Protection of Individuals with regard to Automatic Processing of Personal Data (ETS No.108) and to the Recommendation No. R (97) 5, as well as to Recommendation No. R (97) 17 on the development and implementation of quality improvement systems in health care;

Bearing in mind the report of the Parliamentary Assembly of the Council of Europe on instruments of citizen participation in representative democracy (Doc. 7781(1977));

Noting the relevance of the World Health Organisation's Health 21 programme for the European region and of its recent policy documents on patients' rights and citizens' participation;

Recalling the Amsterdam Declaration on the Promotion of Patients' Rights in Europe;

Noting that the Ljubljana Charter on Reforming Health Care, endorsed by the WHO, stresses the need for health-care systems which focus on people and allow the 'citizens' voice and choice to influence the way in which health services are designed and operate';

Further noting the importance of the Ottawa Charter for Health Promotion (1986) and the Jakarta Declaration on Leading Health Promotion into the 21st Century (1997) as statements on the guiding principles for public health;

Recognising that a health-care system should be patient-oriented;

Considering that citizens should necessarily participate in decisions regarding their health care;

Recognising the fundamental right of citizens in a free and democratic society to determine the goals and targets of the health-care sector;

Recognising the important role that civic and self-help organisations of patients, consumers, insured persons and citizens play in representing 'users'' interests in health-care and recognising that their primary role is both to provide support and services to and further the interests of their members;

Considering that participation in the decision-making process will lead to public acceptance of health-policy goals;

Considering that it is necessary for each member state to help to broaden the public's general knowledge about health problems, promote healthy living, disease prevention and ways of taking responsibility for their own health;

Recognising the fact that empowering citizens revitalises representative democracy, enhances social cohesion, leads to the better functioning of the health-care system, and establishes a better balance of interests and a partnership between the various players in the system;

Conscious that patient empowerment and citizen participation can be achieved only if basic patients' rights are implemented and that, in its turn, patient participation is a tool for the full implementation of these rights in daily practice;

Recognising that there are different levels of citizens' empowerment, from the ability to influence the overall administration of the health-care system and to participate in the decision-making process, through the ability to further particular interests through organisations of patients or citizens, through representation on boards or executive bodies governing health-care establishments, and through direct influence over the provision of health care through the freedom of choice,

Recommends that the governments of member states:
- ensure that citizens' participation should apply to all aspects of health-care systems, at national, regional and local levels, and should be observed by all health-care system operators, including professionals, insurers and the authorities;
- take steps to reflect in their law the guidelines contained in the appendix to this recommendation;
- create legal structures and policies that support the promotion of citizens' participation and patients' rights, if these do not already exist;
- adopt policies that create a supportive environment for the growth, in membership, orientation and tasks, of civic organisations of health-care 'users', if these do not already exist;
- support the widest possible dissemination of the recommendation and its explanatory memorandum, paying special attention to all individuals and organisations aiming at involvement in decision-making in health care.

116

The Appendix to Recommendation (2000) 5 sets out the following guide lines for member states:

I Citizen and patient participation as a democratic process

The right of citizens and patients to participate in the decision-making process affecting health care, if they wish to do so, must be viewed as a fundamental and integral part of any democratic society. Governments should develop policies and strategies that promote patients' rights and citizens' participation in the decision-making in health care, and provide for their dissemination, monitoring and updating.

Patient/citizen participation should be an integral part of health-care systems and, as such, an indispensable component in current health-care reforms.

Decision-making should be made more democratic by ensuring:

- a clear distribution of responsibilities for decision-making in health care;
- appropriate influence of all interest groups, including civic associations active in health-related matters, and not only of some stakeholders (professionals, insurers, etc.);
- public access to political debates on such issues;
- wherever possible, citizens' participation at the problem identification and policy development stages; participation should not be confined to resolving problems and simply choosing between solutions that have already been drawn up. Public debates should be more widely used to strengthen participatory mechanisms.

II Information

Information on health care and on the mechanisms of the decision-making process should be widely disseminated in order to facilitate participation. It should be easily accessible, timely, easy to understand and relevant.

Governments should improve and strengthen their

117

communication and information strategies should be adapted to the population group they address.

Regular information campaigns and other methods such as information through telephone hotlines should be used to heighten the public's awareness of patients' rights. Adequate referral systems should be put in place for patients who would like additional information (with regard to their rights and existing enforcement mechanisms).

III Supportive policies for active participation

Governments should create an environment that is supportive of people's participation and responsibility in decision-making in health care. This implies: instituting or strengthening mechanisms and/or structures for such participation; listening to patients and citizens should become a constant concern for the whole health-care system at all administrative levels and in all regional, federal or national branches of health authorities; supporting democratic procedures for nominating and selecting citizens' representatives including membership in ethics committees, health boards and advisory bodies or any other structure in charge of taking health-oriented decisions; involving citizens and health-care users in the management of different structures of the health-care system; introducing ongoing evaluation of the dynamic participatory processes in which citizens and patients take part; ensuring that all relevant population groups are able to participate on an equal basis; eliminating financial, geographical and/or cultural and linguistic restrictions to participation; promoting additional assistance to vulnerable groups to facilitate their participation; endorsing education and training facilities for citizens in order to develop democratic participation.

Governments should adopt policies that create a supportive environment for the growth in membership, orientation and tasks of civic organisations of health-care 'users' by: creating a legal basis for participation of citizens in the management of health-care facilities and insurance companies; creating favourable conditions, both in the legal and fiscal system, for the founding and operating of such organisations; the health budget, as far as possible, should include allocations to support such organisations; creating favourable legal conditions to support financing of such organisations by the industry while avoiding conflicts of interests; stimulating co-operation, whenever possible, between organisations, while respecting their diversity. Citizens' associations dealing with health matters should work together towards achieving alliance strategies; facilitating the provision of services and support by these organisations to as many people as possible; granting these organisations a role in providing information to their members and the general public on specific questions and/or general health information; allowing such organisations their place among other interest groups in health care (organisations of professionals, insurers, etc.); encouraging democratic and ethical debates in these associations; developing transparent and open relationships between public authorities and associations.

The following complementary measures should be envisaged: publishing an annual report on the progress in citizens' participation in the decision-making process affecting health care; ensuring that every contract concluded with the public authorities or between key operators in the health-care system should include a commitment to develop citizen/patient participation; training health professionals in communication and in participation practices; developing, in consultation with the NGOs, research programmes on patient/citizen participation in the process of health research and the most effective mechanisms for ensuring participation in the decision-making processes relating to health care.

IV Participation mechanisms

Citizens should participate throughout the legislative process in health care: in the drafting of laws, in their implementation and follow-up, including future modification procedures. This can be achieved through participation in commissions and public debates, whenever appropriate. Citizens/patients should have the possibility of participating in setting priorities in health care. For this purpose, the various different aspects of priority setting should be clearly explained to ensure responsible and informed participation by citizens. Aims, outcomes and responsibilities attached to these choices must be clearly set out, as well as implications of these choices as regards the allocation of resources, reorganisation of the health system and relations between the different components of the health-care system. Patients' viewpoints and expectations should be taken into account when assessing the quality of health care. Patients should have a say in internal evaluation and should also be involved in external evaluation via patients' associations. Contracts with service providers should contain a binding clause to this effect.

Patients and their organisations should be granted access to adequate mechanisms for enforcement of their rights in individual cases, which could be complemented by a supervision mechanism by an independent body. In order to be effective these mechanisms should have a broad range, providing for forms of conciliation and mediation. Formal complaints procedures should be straightforward and easily accessible. Financial barriers to equal access to these mechanisms should be removed, either by making access free of charge or by subsidising people with low incomes who wish to use them.

Systematic collection and analysis of patients' complaints should be used to gather information on the quality of health care and as an indication for areas and aspects that need improvement.

Annex 4: A Blueprint for Reform and Strengthening of CHCs

Statutory role

CHCs should retain the rights and obligations they have now, but should be accorded some additional, fully funded responsibilities, if they are to be able to fulfil an effective and sustained watchdog role in the NHS. The following additional powers, which would need to be properly resourced, are proposed:

Statutory complaints function
Although CHCs provide support for complainants within the NHS, this is not part of their statutory function, and they are not specifically resourced for it. The recommendations of the health select committee, in November 1999, that the NHS fund an army of properly trained patients' advocates, and base them in CHC offices, should be implemented. Individuals with a complaint should have certain rights to be supported through the complaint, but there would need to be clear safeguards for CHCs and advocates, for example with respect to vexatious complainants.

Statutory role with respect to PCG/PCTs
All CHCs should have the right to speaking observer status on relevant PCG and PCT boards. They should be given the right to place items on the agenda, as well as comment on them. They should be given an official role in supporting the lay members of PCG boards, for example through the provision

of independent information and advice. CHCs should also be given responsibility for carrying out the public involvement role for PCGs/PCTs – effectively having it contracted out to them, so that they become the official bridge between health decision-makers and the local community

Automatic speaking rights at Trust Board and Health Authority meetings
CHC representatives should have the right to attend for Part 2 items. Information should be confidential to the CHC, not the individual representative. Confidentiality should bind CHC members only where they feel that the public interest does not dictate otherwise.
- *Quality function* – e.g., carrying out user-satisfaction surveys.
- *Formal link with Commission for Health Improvement (CHIs)* – with the right to call CHI in for investigation.
- *Enforcement of charter rights when the new NHS Charter is launched.*
- *Possible coverage of the private sector* – rights should follow the patient, not the sector, so that CHCs have inspection rights etc. when NHS patients are treated at the expense of the NHS on private sector premises. Consideration also needs to be given to providing a role for CHCs in the regulation of the private sector.
- *Role in promoting the responsible patient.*
- *Training and remuneration of staff* – need to be regularised so that there are common national standards and rates of pay, linked to common job descriptions.
- *There should be a clear corporate identity for CHCs* (on the Citizens' Advice Bureau model).

CHC members

- There should be mandatory training for CHC members.
- There should be member/chair/vice chair contracts/job descriptions for all CHCs, building on work already done in this area.
- Bring CHC appointments into line with Nolan standards.

- There should be a move away from the current system of Secretary of State appointments.
- Adopt a system of advertisement, paper application and interview, in line with the rest of the public sector. This system already operates for Health Council appointments in Scotland.
- New systems need to address the growing conflict of interest for local councillors with the advent of joint commissioning and the problem that the voluntary sector is increasingly a provider of health services.
- Equal opportunities issues can only be addressed if patronage moves away from the existing power groups of well-established voluntary groups and the political parties.
- CHCs should have proper indemnity/corporate status.
- CHC members should be entitled to time off work for public duties and a right to payment for loss of earnings.
- Other payments for CHC members need to be considered as these increasingly become the norm for other lay positions in the health service (e.g., lay members of Primary Care Groups).

ACHCEW

- *To be centrally funded.*
- *To become standard-setting body for all CHCs* – would include training function, dealing with complaints about CHCs, and some role in member appointments.
- *Additional funding for CHCs for non-core activities could be linked to ACHCEW accreditation.*
- *The functions of an enhanced ACHCEW would include*:
- The provision of information and legal services to CHCs;
- Liaising with government and national bodies within the NHS on behalf of CHCs;
- Providing mandatory training to all CHC members;
- Set standards for CHCs and enforce them;
- Acting as a clearing house for the work of CHCs in monitoring local services, so that lessons can be learnt and best practice identified in health service delivery.
- *ACHCEW should, as a statutory body, report to the*

Secretary of State, either directly or through an appointed board of trustees (cf. Commission for Racial Equality/ Equal Opportunities Commission model). The Board of trustees should include people with a proven record of involvement with CHCs. Continuity between any new board and the existing lay structures of ACHCEW would also be important.

- *Regional associations of CHCs should become regional associations of ACHCEW.* They are currently stand-alone Associations, although their representatives make up the current ruling body of ACHCEW. They should be properly staffed as regional offices of the Association. There also needs to be a properly resourced Welsh office of ACHCEW – with significantly enhanced staffing in the light of devolution.
- *Wider reference group of CHCs.* In order to ensure that any reconfigured ACHCEW remained responsive to the grass-roots needs of CHCs, a wider reference group of CHC representatives would need to be established to advise the director and trustees.

Other future options for the Association would be for:
- *ACHCEW to become a Special Health Authority.*
- *ACHCEW to report to a Select Committee.*

ANNEX 5: PUBLIC OPINION AND THE NHS

THE COMMISSION COMMISSIONED an opinion poll on attitudes towards the NHS so that our recommendations could be founded on the views of the public. ICM interviewed a random sample of 1,004 adults aged eighteen and over by telephone between 24 and 26 March 2000. Interviews were conducted across the country and the results have been weighted to the profile of all adults.

Respondents were first asked to choose 'the most valuable institution for this country' from a list of seven institutions. The institutions were ranked in this order: the NHS was the most popular with 63 per cent of those polled; Parliament followed on 12 per cent, then the police (11 per cent), the BBC (4 per cent), the Royal Family (3 per cent), and the Bank of England and Benefits Agency (2 per cent each). Don't-knows amounted to 4 per cent. The police received most second preferences (44 per cent), followed by the NHS (17 per cent) and Parliament (14 per cent).

Respondents were then asked which of seven traditional human rights and three social rights should be included in a Bill of Rights. The scores were as follows: the right to privacy in your own home, 99 per cent; the right to free speech, 98 per cent; the right to vote in regular elections for the government of this country, 97 per cent; the right to free medical treatment at the time of need, 96 per cent; the right to practise your religion without state interference, 95 per cent; the right to a fair trial before a jury, 92 per cent; the right to free assembly for peaceful meetings or demonstrations, and the right to know what information government departments hold on you, 90 per cent each; the right of those who are homeless to be rehoused, 84 per cent; the right of a woman to have an abortion, 80 per cent. Only on four of these rights did a significant number say that the right should not be included: 14 per cent opposed the right to abortion, 10 per cent opposed a right to be rehoused, 7 per cent opposed both the right of assembly and the right of individuals to know what information government holds on them.

As stated in the Executive Summary, 67 per cent of respondents agreed that the NHS needs a constitution of its own to define the government's duty to deliver free medical care at a time when people need it; and 26 per cent agreed that the public should trust elected politicians in government to safeguard the NHS's performance of that duty. There were 5 per cent don't-knows.

The public views on the state of the NHS are fully reported in the Executive Summary. There were only 1 per cent don't-knows. Asked about the responsiveness of the NHS, 56 per cent agreed that the NHS is 'remote from the public and hard to influence'; 36 per cent agreed with the contrary view that it is run 'in an open way and consults the public'. Don't-knows: 8 per cent.

ICM's pollsters gave people four choices for the running of health authorities locally. The scores were as follows: a committee of the local authority, 8 per cent; a government-appointed committee, 11 per cent; a committee elected directly by local people, 34 per cent; a committee which is partly elected, partly appointed, 41 per cent. Don't-knows: 7 per cent.

The last two questions concerned people's views about their power over the medical treatment they received: how much power did they have, and how much power should they and other patients have. The following table shows the results:

	The power people believe they have (%)	The power people believe they should have (%)
A lot of power	20	55
A little power	51	39
No power at all	22	3
Don't know	7	4

ANNEX 6: SOURCES OF EVIDENCE TO THE COMMISSION

Organisations
Age Concern England
All-Party Parliamentary Group on Community Health
   Councils
AIMS – Association for Improvements in the Maternity
   Services
Bedfordshire Health
Blackburn, Hyndburn and Ribble Valley Health Care NHS
   Trust
British Medical Association (BMA)
Bromley Health Authority
Cheltenham and Gloucester College of Higher Education
City & Hackney Community Services NHS Trust
Communications Forum
Cornwall Healthcare NHS Trust
Dacorum Hospital Action Group
Democratic Health Network
Dorset Health Authority
Dyfed Powys Health Authority
East Kent Community NHS Trust
East Kent Hospitals NHS Trust
General Dental Council
General Medical Council
Harlow Primary Care Group
Kingston and District Community NHS Trust
Liverpool Health Authority
Medical Protection Society

Mencap – the Royal Society for Mentally Handicapped
  Children and Adults
National Aids Trust
National Children's Bureau
National Consumer Council
National Health Service Consultants' Association
NHS Confederation
NHS Cymru Wales/Welsh Office
NHS Executive North West
NHS Executive South East
NHS Support Federation
Norfolk Mental Health Care NHS Trust
North & East Devon Health Authority
North Essex Health Authority
Nottingham City Hospital NHS Trust
Oldham NHS Trust
Oxford City Council
Pain Concern (UK) – Lothian Group
RADAR The Disability Network
RNIB – Royal National Institute for the Blind
Royal College of Anaesthetists
Royal College of General Practitioners
Royal College of Nursing
Royal College of Paediatrics and Child Health
Royal College of Physicians
Salford and Trafford Health Authority
Sefton Council
Sefton Council for Voluntary Service
Sefton Health
The Association of Therapeutic Communities
The Haemophilia Society
The Long-Term Medical Conditions Alliance
The Relatives and Residents Association
The Royal College of General Practitioners
The Royal College of Midwives
The Royal Orthopaedic Hospital NHS Trust
The Royal Society for the Promotion of Health
UKCC – United Kingdom Central Council for Nursing,
  Midwifery and Health Visiting

UKPHA – UK Public Health Association
W.A.T.C.H. – Watford Against Threats to Close Hospitals
West Hertfordshire Health Authority
West Kent Health Authority
West Surrey Health Authority
West Sussex Health Authority
Weston Area Health Trust

Individuals

Alan Bedford
Albert Weale
Caroline Nichols
Evelyn Mc Ewen
Guy Daly, Howard Davis
John Pearson
John Walsh
Lynda Bagley
Margaret Tozer
Martyn Smith
Mick Rolfe, Howard Lawes, Denise Holden
M. C. T. Morrison
Steve Turner

Terry Ewington
Mr & Mrs Pillai
Donald Roy
Chris Dabbs
Bill Oxburgh
Anne Damerell
Jean Brett
Dr Patrick Logan
Richard Rawlins
Cllr Dick Anthony
Sir Christopher Foster
Mike Rowe
Dr Doug Naysmith
Lesley Stuart

Community Health Councils

Airedale
Anglesey – Ynys Mon
Association of West Midlands CHCs
Association of Welsh CHCs
Barnsley
Basingstoke & North Hampshire
Bath & District
Bristol & District
Bromley
Bury
Cambridge
Canterbury and Thanet

Central Lincolnshire
CHC Development Association
Cheshire Central
Chester & Ellesmere Port
Chorley & South Ribble
Croydon
Coventry
Darlington and Teesdale
Dewsbury District
Doncaster
Dudley
East Birmingham
East Dorset

East Herts
East Suffolk
Exeter and District
Eastern Regional
  Association
Great Yarmouth and
  Waveney District
Greenwich
Gloucestershire
Haringey
Harrogate & District
Hillingdon
Huntingdon
Isles of Scilly
Kensington & Chelsea and
  Westminster
Kidderminster and District
Leeds
Leicestershire
Lewisham
Medway & Swale
Mid Downs
Newcastle
Northallerton District
North Bedfordshire
North Birmingham
North East Essex
North East Wales
North East Warwickshire
North Devon
North Gwent
Northamptonshire North
North Staffordshire
North Tyneside
North West Anglia
North West Regional
  Association
North West Surrey
Oxfordshire

Plymouth and District
Pontefract and District
Portsmouth & South East
  Hants
Preston
Regional Association of
  London CHCs
Richmond and Twickenham
Salford
Scarborough & North East
  Yorkshire
Sheffield
Society of CHC Staff
Solihull
South Birmingham
South Durham & Weardale
South East Regional
  Association of
  Community Health
  Councils
South Sefton
South Warwickshire
South West Association of
  Community Health
  Councils
South West Surrey
Somerset
Southend District
Southern Derbyshire
Swindon & District
Tameside & Glossop
Torbay & District
Tower Hamlets
Trafford
Trent Regional Association
  of CHCs
Wakefield
West Dorset
West Essex

West Midlands Association
  of Chief Officers
West Suffolk
West Surrey & North East
  Hampshire
Winchester & Central
  Hampshire
Worcester District

132